JOURI **)LOGY**

| Volume 4, Number 2 | 1998 |

SPECIAL ISSUE: PEACE BY FORCEFUL MEANS?

SUBSCRIBER INFORMATION

Peace and Conflict: Journal of Peace Psychology is published four times a year and is available on a calendar-year basis only. In the United States and Canada, per-volume rates are US $35 for individuals and US $140 for institutions; in other countries, per-volume rates are US $65 for individuals and US $170 for institutions. Send subscription orders and information requests to the Journal Subscription Department, Lawrence Erlbaum Associates, Inc., 10 Industrial Avenue, Mahwah, NJ 07430–2262.

Address changes: Members of Division 48 of the APA should contact Adele Schaefer, Division Services Office, APA, 750 First St. NE, Washington DC 20002–4242. Direct subscribers should contact Lawrence Erlbaum Associates, Inc., at the aforementioned address. Address changes should include the mailing label or a facsimile. Claims for missing issues cannot be honored beyond 4 months after mailing date. Duplicate copies cannot be sent to replace issues not delivered due to failure to notify publisher of change of address.

This journal is abstracted or indexed in *PsycINFO/Psychological Abstracts.* Microform copies of this journal are available through UMI, Periodical Check-In, North Zeeb Road, P.O. Box 1346, Ann Arbor, MI 48106–1346.

Special requests for permission should be addressed to Permissions Department, Lawrence Erlbaum Associates, Inc., 10 Industrial Avenue, Mahwah, NJ 07430–2262.

PEACE AND CONFLICT: JOURNAL OF PEACE PSYCHOLOGY, 4(2), 89–91

Introduction: Peace by Forceful Means?

Milton Schwebel

Graduate School of Applied and Professional Psychology
Rutgers University

Peace by Peaceful Means, the title of Johan Galtung's (1997) book, expresses a centuries-old hope of humankind. This planet of ours has witnessed enough brutality for its lifetime. Let there be peace, and let it be accomplished strictly by peaceful means.

Those who take a long-term view of history have reason to believe that the hope of humankind is justified. In an article in the first issue of this journal, Federico Mayor (1995), Director General of United Nations Educational, Scientific, and Cultural Organization (UNESCO), said that the journal was born at a moment in history that "offers us an unprecedented opportunity to break with the culture of war and pursue a new path toward a culture of peace" (p. 3). Three years ago, the Culture of Peace Program was one feature of UNESCO's activities. Now, the United Nations (UN), itself, has adopted it to the extent that the year 2000 will be the United Nations' Year of a Culture of Peace.

Once regarded as a sickly colt that had about as much chance of survival as the League of Nations, after half a century, the UN has become a permanent feature of international life. That its success has been far less than we would have wished does not detract from the desirability of envisioning a peaceful world and the wisdom of striving for peace by peaceful means.

To psychologists and other social and behavioral scientists and the respective practitioners in those fields, that goal—peace by peaceful means—is entirely compatible with their theories of human consciousness and conduct. Yes, conflict is inevitable in all human affairs, in the relationships among people whether in families, schools, workplaces, or the community at large. Although efforts to eliminate some of the sources of conflict may reduce its incidence, nothing in our understanding of human behavior leads us to believe that conflict per se can ever,

---

Requests for reprints should be sent to Milton Schwebel, Graduate School of Applied and Professional Psychology, Rutgers University, 152 Frelinghuysen Road, Piscataway, NJ 08854–8085. E-mail: mschwebe@rci.rutgers.edu

or even should ever, be eradicated. Our fields have developed creative, nonviolent means of resolving conflicts that already are proving useful in curbing violence under circumstances that usually lead to tragic consequences. The timing of their development is noteworthy.

Historically, these peaceful means of conflict resolution have emerged on the world stage at a moment when the people and many governments have concluded that warfare as an instrument of political power between nations is retrogressive and must be made obsolete. Today, interstate wars hardly figure on that world stage.

By contrast, the violence reported in our media is about intrastate and interpersonal conflict: Ethnic, racial, or religious groups vying with each other for land or jobs or political power or human and civil rights. Women and girls abused and brutalized by one means or another. Some of this violence is a consequence of societal structures that unnecessarily delimit opportunities, for example, for work or for political equality, or that deny equal rights to various categories of people, especially women. These circumstances, too, can be ameliorated, and the conflicts can be subjected to peaceful modes of resolution.

Even the single greatest danger on earth, the 35,000 nuclear weapons that remain in the world, can now be eliminated, as Jonathan Schell (1998) has written convincingly in his essay, "The Gift of Time: The Case for Abolishing Nuclear Weapons." Many military and other leaders who had been responsible for nuclear policy during the cold war now favor the global elimination of nuclear weapons, "a position unthinkable for them even a decade ago" (p. 16). According to Schell, abolition of the weapons is possible today not only because the cold war circumstances that were used to justify their need no longer exist but also, quoting the words of Jody Williams, expressed on the day her campaign to ban landmines led to a treaty signed by 121 nations, because "together we are a superpower. It's a new definition of superpower. It's not one of us; it's all of us" (p.16).

Taken together, we have reason to hope for and struggle for a world that resolves conflict by peaceful means. Nevertheless, the current reality, evident in daily media reports, is that violence is a fact of everyday life. Those horrible weapons exist, always an unsettling threat, even as the cold war greatly reduced our anxiety about them. In addition, bloody violence in one form or another in every corner of our planet has become so commonplace that we become hardened to it and listen to the numbers of victims as if they were reports of sporting event scores. Even as we struggle to achieve the civilized status of using peaceful means to maintain the peace, we must not deny the grim realities of life today.

Those current realities demand that we pay attention to Ralph White's views on the use of force in maintaining the peace, whether or not we end up agreeing with him. In fact, he wants dialogue not agreement. After accepting his article for publication, I asked him how he would feel if I invited several people to comment on it. His immediate response was favorable: "Yes, that's a good idea. But make sure you get critics who differ with me!"

This veteran psychologist, whom most of us first became acquainted with through the landmark study on authoritarian, democratic, and laissez-faire methods of group leadership by Lewin, Lippitt, and White (1939), won't be disappointed. Political scientist Jack Levy and psychologists George Loevenger, Ethel Tobach, and Richard Wagner, all of them admirers of White's lifetime devotion to the struggle for peace, have not hesitated to take different positions from his. On behalf of the Peace Division of the American Psychological Association, I thank them all for their contributions to this important debate.

REFERENCES

Galtung, J. (1997). *Peace by peaceful means: Peace and conflict, development and civilization.* London: Sage.

Lewin, K., Lippitt, R., & White, R. K. (1939). Patterns of aggressive behavior in experimentally created "social climates." *Journal of Social psychology, 10,* 271–299.

Mayor, F. (1995). How psychology can contribute to a culture of peace. *Peace and Conflict: Journal of Peace Psychology, 1,* 3–10.

Schell, J. (1998). The gift of time: The case for abolishing nuclear weapons. *The Nation, 266,* 9–60.

This general lack of active concern, indeed, near apathy toward the bomb, seems to stem primarily from a feeling of helplessness, a belief that there is little or nothing the individual can do about the problem... In addition to being informed about the bomb, people must not only see the possibility of constructive action, but must also see what they as individuals can do to help solve the problem.

Patricia Woodward, 1948

PEACE AND CONFLICT: JOURNAL OF PEACE PSYCHOLOGY, *4*(2), 93–128

American Acts of Force: Results and Misperceptions

Ralph K. White
Cockeysville, Maryland

This article examines and evaluates the apparent results of 12 prominent examples of American acts of force ranging from its entry into World War I to North American Treaty Organization's (NATO) massive air strike that ended the war in Bosnia. The values in terms of which I judge them are military success (to the extent that it promotes other values), low cost (in loss of life, physical suffering, and economic deprivation), peace (ending or avoiding a war), international good will, democracy, and freedom from alien rule. With 6, I judge to have had mainly "good" results: World War II in Europe, World War II in Asia, the defense of South Korea, the Berlin Crisis, the Cuban Missile Crisis, and the Bosnian War. This study rates 4 to have had mainly "bad" results: the invasion of North Korea, the Bay of Pigs, the Vietnam War, and the SAC Alert in 1973. Two were ambiguous in this respect: World War I and the Persian Gulf War. Separately, this article judges negatively the results of many lesser interventions and the results of the excessive buildup of nuclear arms. The results of the Cold War are evaluated positively for the Stalin period but more negatively than positively for the entire period since his death, 1953–1989. Using a modified form of Levy's (1983) terminology, I associate 5 misperceptions with bad results: a demonized enemy image, an idealized self-image, overconfidence, underconfidence, and absence of realistic empathy (with opponents or third parties). This article suggests some guidelines for future policy.

Historians and political scientists have devoted an enormous amount of attention to studying the causes of war. There are a great many studies of the causes of individual wars, such as Luigi Albertini's (1952–1957) three-volume work on the immediate causes of World War I. There is the highly quantitative study of the *Correlates of War* by the Michigan group headed by J. David Singer (1972). There is the comprehensive essay "The Causes of War: A Review of Theories and Evidence" by Jack Levy (1989), which contains 427 citations.

Requests for reprints should be sent to Ralph K. White, 13801 York Road, Cockeysville, MD 21030–1825.

They have given little systematic attention, however, to war's results or to the effectiveness of threats of war. A broad evidence-based study of the uses or threats of force on the international level would be hard to find. A partial exception is the Brookings study, *Force Without War* by Blechman and Kaplan (1978).

Results do matter. It would be useful to have some answers—even rough, tentative answers—to practical questions such as the following: Are the advocates of nonviolence right when they believe that almost any use or threat of international force is likely to do more harm than good? In America's experience, under what circumstances has its use of international threat or actual use of force had mainly good rather than bad results? What misperceptions have tended to promote the unwise and unrealistic use of force, judging by results?

This article seeks what must necessarily be rough and tentative answers to these questions. The 12 prominent examples of American acts of force focus on whether these have had "good" or "bad" results. However, what do good and bad mean?

For whom is a particular result good? In terms of what more specific values?

Two questions call for answers: *Good for whom?* This article defines good as when the result is good for the greatest number of those affected. This is an internationalist criterion. The welfare of a German, a Russian, an Iraqi, or a Serb is given as much weight as that of an American.

There is an alternative basic value criterion, enlightened national self-interest. In practice, there is little difference between this and the internationalist criterion I use. On this tiny and shrinking planet, the welfare of each depends to a considerable extent on the welfare of others. Wars tend to spread, war refugees overflow national boundaries, diseases spread, drugs spread, and cooperation among nations is essential if such planetary problems are to be effectively handled. The reader who leans toward enlightened self-interest as the basic criterion may be surprised to find how many of the specific value judgments in this article he or she agrees with.

The six values chiefly utilized for judgments in this article are (a) military success to the extent that it leads to the satisfaction of other human needs; (b) low cost in terms of death, physical suffering, and economic deprivation; (c) peace, in the form of ending or avoiding a war; (d) international goodwill and cooperation; (e) democracy, defined as human rights combined with majority rule; and (f) national independence, defined as absence of alien rule. Each of these is discussed in somewhat more detail next.

SIX CRITERIA OF GOOD RESULTS

Military Success

The term *military success* covers both victory in war and, in the case of threats, achieving the purpose of the threat.

From an internationalist standpoint (which is mine) military success is not necessarily a positive value. Victory for one country always means defeat for another, and enhanced relative power for one means increased weakness for another. There is a special danger in what Fulbright (1966) referred to as the arrogance of power at a time when the United States is the only superpower. Such arrogance may lead to military overconfidence, which, as we shall see, has been a main cause of war.

This study, however, suggests that, in our century, American military success and consequent power have served basic human values (peace, goodwill, democracy, and national independence) more than their opposites (war, ill will, autocracy, and national subjugation). They will, therefore, be considered in this context good rather than bad. Hans Morgenthau (1967), an immensely influential student of international politics, has a similar conception of the relation of power to other ends, good and bad. He describes power as the currency of the international sphere, much as money is the currency of the economic sphere. In any case, power, like money, is an important fact to recognize as is military success for its relation to power.

I, therefore, begin my description of the findings of the study with a summary of America's military success and two factors associated with it (see Table 1).

Defense is an action to protect a country (which may be one's own) from an ongoing offensive action by another. An *offensive action* is defined as use or threat of force in foreign territory, against the probable wishes of a majority of the people in that territory.

World support is defined to include fighting allies, general moral support by world opinion, or official support by transnational organizations such as the United Nations (UN) and North American Treaty Organization (NATO). As such, it may reflect the actual fact of a strong moral position of one's own nation, which has

TABLE 1
Two Conditions Related to Military Success

Event	Use or Threat	Defense?	World Support?	Military Success
World War I	Use	Yes	Yes	Yes
World War II, Europe	Use	Yes	Yes	Yes
World War II, Asia	Use	Yes	Yes	Yes
Korean War, 1st Phase	Use	Yes	Yes?	Yes
Korean War, 2nd Phase	Use	No?	No?	No?
Bay of Pigs	Use	No	No	No
Berlin Crisis	Threat	Yes	Yes	Yes
Missile Crisis	Threat	No?	No?	Yes
Vietnam War	Use	No	No	No
SAC Alert, 1973	Threat	No	No	Yes
Persian Gulf War	Use	Yes	Yes?	Yes
Bosnian War	Use	Yes	Yes	Yes

already produced good fighting spirit, and it may then promote additional war morale in one's own country and its allies while detracting from that of its adversaries. These two relatively objective factors, the defensive role of the United States and the support of its action by "the world," apparently have a surprisingly close relation to military success. One can only speculate on the reasons for this, but the speculation is worthwhile. The defensive role is probably related to success in two ways. When America enters an ongoing war, it automatically has the support of the nations who are already fighting on the same side with strong motivation to defend their homeland (Britain, France, Russia, China). Most of the uses or threats of force by the United States ended in military success—9 out of 12. This could probably be expected of a country as strong as the United States. In fact, the three cases of losing—the second phase of the Korean War, the Bay of Pigs, and the Vietnam War—are probably more surprising and interesting.

There is poetic justice here in that, when America was attacking others, it lost—three times out of four; when it was defending others, it consistently won. It is almost as if we were witnessing an old-fashioned morality play.

Actually, moral considerations probably did play a significant role. Condemnation of war makers and aggressors is now nearly worldwide, even if sometimes insincere. Any nation that appears to be a war maker and an aggressor is likely to be branded the Bad Guy by all hitherto disinterested observers, and, if they intervene, it is likely to be partly because of real moral indignation. However, surely, simple fear (threat perception) is likely to be a more potent motive. For instance, in the second phase of the Korean War, MacArthur invaded North Korea, and the Chinese intervened against him. China had ample reason to intervene to maintain a buffer territory, keeping a strong and hostile nation—the United States—from controlling territory just the other side of the Yalu River from China itself.

Low Cost

Cost is defined here as including loss of life, physical suffering, economic deprivation, and the many acute anxieties connected with being a homeless, hopeless refugee. For example, after the NATO air strike in Bosnia, there were virtually no American casualties and few other casualties.

Peace

Peace is defined here as ending a war, hastening the end of a war, deterring an attack that would otherwise precipitate a war, and avoiding war by skillful negotiation that may include a threat of force. For example, the end of the Bosnian War is again a prime example, and the resolution of the Cuban Missile Crisis is another.

Goodwill and Cooperation

Goodwill can be simply defined as caring about the welfare of others. However, in practice, it includes many things. Negatively, it includes absence of exaggerated fear, hatred, acute rivalry for power, expansionism, or obsessive clinging to national sovereignty. Positively, it includes international friendliness; compassion where needed; generosity; willingness to cooperate actively in causes such as environmental preservation, crime and drug control, population control, and so on; and (as I see it) willingness to work actively for enforceable world or regional law.

For example, whereas a war itself almost necessarily creates intensified ill will in the opponent, it may solidify goodwill with others fighting on the same side against a common enemy. For instance, America's fighting, along with Britain and France in both World Wars, must have solidified good relations with both countries that continued throughout the Cold War and that promoted continual good communication among the three—Britain, France, and the United States.

Democracy

Democracy is defined as human rights, especially freedom of expression and majority rule. For example, the end of World War II seems to have led to the transformation of fairly autocratic societies into much more democratic ones in both Germany and Japan.

National Independence

National independence is defined here not as absence of interdependence (which is often highly desirable) but simply as absence of subjugation of one nation by another. This is not only that freedom from alien rule is and should be an end in itself but also that it represents the well-established balance-of-power principle. For example, after World War II, independence from Nazi rule was restored in many countries.

CASE STUDIES

America's Participation in World War I, 1917–1918

Without America's participation, Britain and France might very well have lost the war. In the Second Battle of the Marne in the summer of 1918, the Germans came as close to winning as they did in 1914. Fresh American troops helped the Allies to win, and by September, 1918, the German cause became hopeless. America's entry into the war was probably the chief reason why a long and ghastly war ended just 2 months later.

The story of the Versailles Treaty and the reaction to it in Germany is well-known. What is not well-known, except in Germany, is the way in which the onset of the War in 1914 enhanced the anger of the Germans against the Versailles Treaty.

In an extreme example of the idealized self-image that tends to exist on both sides of all wars, most of the German people and their rulers felt innocent of any guilt in 1914. Whereas the British, French, and Russians saw the German and Austrian attack on Serbia, and the German attack on France through Belgium, as obviously the acts of aggression that started the war, the Germans saw just the opposite. In their eyes, their "firm handling of Serbia" was necessary to keep the murderous Serbs from initiating the disintegration of Austria–Hungary, which the Serbs were leading, and which in their eyes was being masterminded by Russia. Austria–Hungary was also Germany's only reliable ally; if it disintegrated, Germany would be left alone in a hostile Europe. In German eyes, the attack on France through Belgium was necessitated by the imminence of an invasion from the east by the enormous Czarist Russian empire. Russia and France had been holding Germany in a vise, and a war on two fronts was necessary; France was the one that might be defeated first before turning to repulse the Russian invasion.

This feeling of innocence made the German people feel that the Treaty of Versailles was not only harsh but atrociously unjust. The Germans were being punished for the war by those who had actually perpetrated the crime of war.

This feeling of innocence was something that the British, French, and Americans at the Paris Peace Conference hardly recognized at all. There was little or no realistic empathy with the righteous indignation that almost all Germans felt. Not seeing it, they could and did, with a clear conscience, inflict the Versailles Treaty on the Germans. The passions and largely mistaken images engendered by the war in all those who participated in it continued after the war ended and poisoned the atmosphere of the interwar period. Specifically, Americans themselves were influenced by this enough to inhibit what might have been more constructive action in the 1920s and 1930s. Perhaps such action would have prevented Hitler's rise to power, the Holocaust, and World War II itself.

How do we know that these momentous and tragic events would *not* have occurred if there had been no harsh Versailles Treaty and if there had been, instead, an equivalent of the Marshall Plan, helping both France and Germany get on their feet economically? Of course, we cannot know for sure. We must be on guard against over-speculative "counterfactual thinking" and the fallacy of *post hoc ergo propter hoc* (after this, therefore because of this). It is quite conceivable that the ego trip of the German people, which began with the victory of Prussia over Austria in 1866, plus their semiparanoid siege mentality that began in earnest when Russia loosely joined the Triple Entente in 1907 and that blossomed under Hitler, might have similarly blossomed even if a Marshall Plan had taken the place of the Versailles Treaty.

However, there was an obvious organic connection between the harsh treaty and German resentment, between German resentment and Hitler's rise to power, and between his rise to power and both the Holocaust and World War II. It seems to me that these connections are clear enough to make it probable that nothing as disastrous as what did happen would have occurred if Germany had been treated as humanely after World War I as it was after World War II. In addition, Germany would have been treated more humanely if the Allies had empathized realistically with the Germans' feeling of innocence throughout World War I.

Good Results: A long and ghastly war was ended. Much of Europe was saved from the alien rule of a militaristic Germany. The prestige of democracy as contrasted with both German and Russian hypocrisy was probably enhanced throughout the world.

Bad Results: The demonizing of Germany that led to the Treaty of Versailles and its long-term disastrous consequences.

Chief American Misperception: The demonized image of Germany.

Chief Sources: Albertini (1952), Fay (1966), Fischer (1967), Levy (1989), Schmitt (1958), Tuchman (1962), Keynes (1921), Wolfers (1940), and see White (1949).

World War II in Europe, 1941–1945

Without America's participation, Germany might well have won the war. The broad story of the war is well-known, but many of us may tend to forget how close to victory Germany appeared to be in the dark winter of 1942–43. With German troops in Africa and besieging Stalingrad in the southeastern corner of European Russia, it looked as if a great German pincer movement around the eastern Mediterranean and Black Sea might succeed. The troops in Africa and in Russia might join together and dominate the entire Middle East.

Good Results: The restoration or preservation of independence in a large number of countries including Britain, France, and Russia. The fostering of the growth of a solid democracy in Germany, contrasting with the shaky democracy of the 1920s. The easy coming together of a democratic Germany with the other western powers against the perceived danger of a Soviet invasion. The establishment thereby of the core of the "club" of economically advanced, educated, democratic nations within which, during the entire period since 1945, there has been no war or threat of war.

Bad Results: The war was expensive for America, and many thousands of American lives were lost. However, prosperity continued; there were many who believed that the war "revived the American economy," and the lives lost were not remotely comparable to those lost by the Soviet Union or Germany.

Chief American Misperception: At first, failure to understand Hitler's high flown expansionist ambitions.

Chief Sources: Heiden (1944), Hitler (1943), Shirer (1941), Smith (1942), Taylor (1961). On misperception in this war, see also White (1949).

World War II in Asia, 1941–1945

Without America's very active participation, Japan might have won the whole Far East. Again, the broad story of the war is well-known, but many may not realize how close Japan came to winning it. According to Barbara Tuchman (1970), the Japanese were close to winning the war on the mainland of China when American naval and air superiority finally led to their downfall.

Good Results: America won. Freedom from oppressive alien rule was established for China, Korea, and the southeastern Asian states. Democracy was established and has flourished in Japan. Although not part of its core, Japan, as a prosperous, democratic, and very important state, partially joined the club of states that has not even approached war among itself since 1945.

Bad Results: The war in the Pacific was also expensive and also took many thousands of American lives.

Chief American Misperception: At first, not fully recognizing Japan's territorial ambition.

Chief Sources: Toland (1970), Tuchman (1970).

First Phase of the Korean War, 1950

Kim Il Sung, Communist ruler of North Korea, and Syngman Rhee, strong man of South Korea under American auspices, had each for several years shown signs of wanting to unify the country on his own terms. However, it was Kim Il Sung who actually attacked in force in June, 1950. He already controlled most of South Korea when General MacArthur won a brilliant victory at Inchon.

Although the American Secretary of State, Dean Acheson, had defined all of Korea as outside "the American defense perimeter," President Truman perceived the North Korean attack as flagrant aggression because it crossed the line dividing the Communist from the non-Communist world that had been established in 1945. He felt that it would be appeasement and an encouragement of similar Communist aggression elsewhere if the attack were allowed to succeed.

Good Results: Independence for South Korea. Re-emphasizing the importance of neither side crossing "the Line."

Bad Results: War casualties.

Chief American Misperception: None.

Chief Sources: Acheson (1969), Whiting (1960).

The Invasion of North Korea, 1950–1953

There is such a thing as the momentum of war (c.f. Deutsch 1986). That momentum, plus the exhilaration at General MacArthur's victory at Inchon, carried the United States in October, 1950, across the line that had separated the Communist from the non-Communist worlds. There were also plausible, rational reasons for crossing it: For instance, Communist troops were fleeing in great disarray; militarily this was the time to finish them off.

There was one great omission in this thinking, however: It contained little or no realistic empathy with the Chinese. Truman, Acheson, and MacArthur apparently did not seriously ask themselves what they would do if they were in the situation Mao Tse-Tung and Chou En-Lai were in. They must have perceived America's crossing the line as depriving them of valuable buffered territory between themselves and a very powerful and very hostile United States.

The American decision makers' lack of empathy was not for want of fair warning. As Alexander George and Richard Smoke (1974) have convincingly shown, the Chinese had desperately tried to warn the United States against this blunder.

The results of America's not listening were tragic. The Chinese skillfully infiltrated great numbers of troops across the Yalu; General MacArthur was fatuously overconfident and unprepared to handle them. General Ridgway did a fine job of handling the American retreat, but the Americans did have to retreat, and the war lasted for more than another 2 years. Tens of thousands of American lives and far larger numbers of Chinese and North Korean lives were lost. The war ended just about where it had started.

The Korean War, as a whole, was almost a laboratory experiment in the futility of offensive action and the reasons for its failure. When the Communists took offensive action, they were defeated because of the intervention of a third party, America. When the Americans took offensive action, they were defeated because of the intervention of a third party, China.

From a planetary point of view, the Korean War, as a whole, apparently had good results. When the Communists crossed the line, they burned their fingers and did not attempt the same thing again; when the Americans crossed the line, they burned their fingers and did not attempt the same thing again.

In fact, although few in the West seem to realize it, the Communist world has not crossed the line since Stalin's shift toward a more moderate policy in 1951 (Shulman, 1965). The crackdowns on Hungary and Czechoslovakia were on their side of the line. They backed down on Berlin and Cuba. Even in Afghanistan, which was already ambiguously within their sphere, the motives were quite clearly more defensive than offensive (Garthoff, 1985).

Good Results: Both sides were almost completely deterred from crossing the line that separated them from then on. There were no wars, even small ones, between the two super powers that might have become World War III.

Bad Results: The American invasion prolonged the war by nearly 3 years, increasing the casualties greatly, especially among the Chinese and North Koreans. It made America look aggressive. It made America look stupid. It probably exacerbated tension between East and West.

Chief American Misperception: Not empathizing with China's fear.

Chief Sources: Acheson (1969), George and Smoke (1974), Whiting (1960).

The Bay of Pigs, 1961

Batista, the right-wing dictator of Cuba until 1959, became extremely unpopular by that time. He had been supported at first by the United States but not toward the end. Fidel Castro, ensconced in the mountains with some of his faithful followers, conducted a campaign in which he did not describe himself as either a Communist or a Marxist but rather as a believer in democracy, social reform, and opposition to American imperialism. Most of the people apparently preferred Castro to Batista to such an extent that he came to power in an almost bloodless revolution on January 1, 1959.

In power, Castro thoroughly antagonized most of the American people by continuing to denounce American imperialism, by expropriating American property, by promoting leftist revolutions in other Latin American countries, by accepting help from the Soviet Union, and by declaring that he was a Marxist, all of which were interpreted by most Americans as meaning that he had become a tool of Moscow (actually he never became fully subservient to Moscow in thought or in action). John Kennedy, in his presidential campaign of 1960, made vehement opposition to Castro a main point of his campaign. Meanwhile, the director of the Central Intelligence Agency (CIA), Allen Dulles, was organizing and training Cuban escapees with the possibility in mind of their returning to Cuba as conquerors. Although the last credible opinion poll conducted in Cuba in 1960 registered a large majority in favor of Castro and although State Department intelligence corroborated this, Dulles apparently disbelieved it and clung to the thought that, if a revolution could be touched off by well organized emigré Cubans, a very sizable proportion of the people would come over to the opposition.

When Kennedy came into power, he discovered all the preparations that had been made. He was dubious about going ahead with it, but he did so on the understanding that there would be no public evidence of American involvement. Therefore, it happened.

The result was a fiasco. The Cuban emigrés were quickly captured by Castro's forces, and American involvement had, in the meantime, become transparent. It was a humiliating experience, but Kennedy publicly took the responsibility on himself and probably derived some benefit from doing so because his popularity actually went up in the polls after the fiasco.

Good Results: Practically none.

Bad Results: The unfortunate emigrés now remained in Castro's hands. The incident may well have increased Khrushchev's readiness to take risks 1.5 years later when the Cuban Missile Crisis occurred. The incident made the United States look aggressive. It made the United States look foolish. It made the United States look deceptive because of the transparency of the mask of United States noninvolvement.

Chief American Misperception: Demonizing Castro.

Chief Sources: Cantril (1967), Smith (1987).

The Berlin Crisis, 1958–1962

The Earth is dotted with ulcerous spots: Northern Ireland, Alsace-Lorraine, the Sudetenland, the Polish Corridor, Bosnia, Kosovo, Macedonia, the Ogaden, Israel and Palestine (especially Jerusalem and the West Bank), Lebanon, the Shatt al-Arab, Kuwait, Kashmir, and Taiwan. In each of them, one people's territorial self-image overlaps another people's territorial self-image. This creates a conflict that is peculiarly difficult to resolve. West Berlin was one of these spots.

From a Western point of view, shared by the inhabitants of West Berlin, it was a gallant little island of freedom surrounded by a continually threatening world of Communist oppression. From a Communist point of view, it was a natural, integral part of East Germany unnaturally placed under the rule of temporary alien powers by the Potsdam Agreement with no intention that the arrangement would be permanent. It was a hotbed of espionage and of hate-creating subversive propaganda, inciting a rebellion that could spread by way of a domino process to all of East Europe and depriving the Soviet Union of buffer territory protecting it from another capitalist assault. Moreover, it was the location of a severe hemorrhage of competent people escaping from East Germany through West Berlin to the West.

This became serious in 1961 and was steadily increasing at the time of greatest crisis. It was weakening and harming the economy of East Germany.

These fears had a solid basis in fact. Berlin probably was a center of espionage, and it certainly was a center of anti-Communist persuasion. Radio In the American Sector (RIAS) was an exceptionally effective provider of information and a catalyst of anti-Communist feeling. It did, in effect, create a psychological basis for an anti-Communist rebellion that could easily have spread and become a domino process for rebellion in the whole area.

The Berlin Crisis of 1958–1962 came and went intermittently, reaching a climax just before the Berlin Wall went up in August, 1961. Khrushchev insistently asserted that, unless a better agreement could be reached, he would sign a peace treaty with East Germany that would end the ties of Berlin with the West.

President Kennedy, after a bungling beginning, handled the crisis well in his summit meeting with Khrushchev in Vienna. He demonstrated resolve by beefing up U.S. troops in Berlin, by substantially increasing the military budget, and by visiting Berlin, during which visit he declared to thunderous applause, "Ich Bin ein Berliner" (I am a Berliner). At the same time, he made one concession that may have been essential. Letting Khrushchev know what reaction to expect when the Berlin Wall went up, he denounced it but used no military force to prevent it. In effect, he tacitly agreed to it. The result was an end to the crisis.

Good Results: Peace was preserved. There was no real appeasement. The hemorrhage of people was stopped, and the East German economy stabilized. The importance of not crossing the line separating the Communist from the non-Communist world was reasserted.

Bad Results: None

Chief American Misperception: Not recognizing Khrushchev's fears and consequently having a still demonized image of him.

Chief Sources: Beschloss (1991), Kennan (1972), Ulam (1971).

The Cuban Missile Crisis, 1962

The so-called Missile Gap, which Kennedy had talked about during his 1960 presidential campaign, had proved to be a myth based on faulty intelligence. The nuclear superiority of the United States at that time was actually enormous. Khrushchev knew this. Also, very recently, aerial recognizance had enabled the United States to pinpoint the launching sites of the missiles in the Soviet Union. This meant that the United States already had a clear first-strike capability. It could destroy the Soviet Union's retaliatory capacity at any time and launch a nuclear war with comparative impunity. Khrushchev apparently believed that having Soviet missiles close to the United States would substantially diminish America's readiness to take advantage of that opportunity.

The fascination of Khrushchev and his colleagues with Cuba, and their desire to protect it, were more a matter of their former positive socialist idealism than redressing the nuclear imbalance of power. For them, Cuba symbolized all their youthful hopes that communism might triumph—spontaneously, democratically—throughout the third world. In 1962, the impracticality of the communist form of socialism had not yet dawned on them. It took Kennedy some time to realize that Khrushchev's indignation at the American Jupiter missiles in Turkey was as justified as his own indignation at the Soviet missiles in Cuba. He had already realized how little the Jupiter missiles in Turkey mattered from the standpoint of American security. Putting these two things together in his mind, he arrived at the obvious legitimate concession he could make to satisfy Khrushchev's most emotional fear. A deal, trading removal of America's missiles in Turkey for removal of Soviet missiles in Cuba, might give him peace without appeasement.

It had to be done secretly because the American people were imbued with the idea that any "rewarding of the aggressor" was appeasement. By way of his brother, Robert Kennedy, and Kennedy's relationship with Soviet Ambassador Dobrynin in Washington, the deal was done. The American people saw the end of the crisis as a pure triumph of firmness over Soviet criminality. However, that was not the whole story. The deal was not publicly known until the late 1980s. Meanwhile, Americans had a deeply satisfying feeling of virility combined with nobility.

Good Results: It did give the world peace without appeasement. Surprisingly, it was followed by a decrease of ill will on both sides that probably paved the way for the Nixon–Kissinger détente of the early 1970s. As Georgi Arbatov (personal communication, June, 1986) later put it to me, "Both sides looked into the abyss and pulled back."

Bad Results: The American people's demonized image of Castro was not diminished and may have been hardened.

Chief American Misperception: Demonized images of both Castro and Khrushchev.

Chief Sources: Allison (1971), Beschloss (1991), Blight, Allyn, and Welch (1993), Kagan (1995).

The Vietnam War, 1965–1975

Surely, most readers are familiar with the events of the Vietnam War, starting with the beginning of America's serious involvement in 1965. We will, therefore, focus on a brief sketch of the previous history and some psychological aspects of American involvement in the war.

Vietnam was under Chinese rule and influence during roughly the first thousand years of the Christian era and proudly independent during most of the succeeding thousand years. It was not conquered by France until the 1870s and 1880s (Buttinger, 1958). French rule was much resented, and during the time when France was in trouble at home during World War II, an independence movement developed under the leadership of Ho Chi Minh, who was a Communist but more basically a nationalist. It triumphed, and a newly independent nation, Vietnam, was announced. The French began then to try to reconquer their lost colony. After 9 difficult years, they lost, much as the United States spent 10 years, 1965–1975, and lost. The essential reason was the same, the fierce and tenacious spirit of a great many of the Vietnamese when they believed that their homeland was being invaded by foreigners.

In 1954, the terms of peace with France included independence of North Vietnam under Ho Chi Minh's rule and a promise that 3 years later, in 1957, there would be a vote in South Vietnam to determine whether it should become part of the same country.

In South Vietnam, Ngo Dinh Diem's nationalism was conservative and strongly anti-Communist. During the next 8 years, 1957–1965, the Communist-oriented Viet Cong became stronger and stronger in the South, receiving some help from the Viet Minh government in the North. It was not an invasion from the North but essentially a civil war within the South. It gathered momentum in spite of CIA involvement and thousands of American "advisors" supporting Diem's government. The perceived danger that the Viet Cong would win became so great by 1965 that the United States intervened with full force.

Now some psychological aspects of America's involvement. First, and most important, is the *demonized enemy image*—a great exaggeration of the villainy of the actual Vietnamese Communists, Viet Minh, and Viet Cong. Jack Levy would call it "an overestimation of the adversary's hostility" (pp. 88–89).

In my view, the exaggeration was greater than in any other of the 12 acts of force in this study because the reality underlying the image was actually relatively good. These Communists were characterized by courage, sincerity, great readiness for self-sacrifice, and intense patriotism. They contrasted greatly with the more purely power-oriented and vindictive Stalinism of Stalin himself. They also contrasted greatly with the corrupt politicians, selfish landowners, usurers, and army officials who constituted the Saigon government that was defended by the United States.

Naturally, they had their own exaggerated, demonized image of the United States, or rather, of the capitalist imperialist "ruling circles" of the United States. It is worthwhile to try to draw up a list of the accusations they might, with some justice, have made against the American role in Vietnam. An imaginary Viet Cong solider might have spoken about the Americans as follows:

They are foreigners, interfering in the domestic affairs of our country. They are imperialists like the French, with whom we battled for our independence for nine years, and finally won. They are against democracy; after promising us a vote to determine whether we could join the North, they broke their promise. They are in league with the landowners and usurers in the cities who have been oppressing us peasants for generations. They are splitters of our country; partly because of them we are tragically divided, north from south. They are war makers. We did not start this war; they did. They are war prolongers. This war could have been ended democratically and quickly if they had allowed us to win in 1965. Instead this horrible war is continuing and continuing. They are users of inhuman methods such as napalm, and their use of torture is far greater than ours. They are hypocrites and liars when they talk about peace and democracy and national independence.

In my view, each of these accusations contains some kernel of truth (White, 1968).

Good Results: Possibly preventing for some years Communist advances elsewhere in Southeast Asia, especially Indonesia.

Bad Results: About 58,000 American deaths. Some 1,500,000 Vietnamese deaths. Prolonging the war by perhaps 8 or 9 years. Very wide-spread opposition elsewhere, except among Vietnam's immediate neighbors. Wounding America's reputation as a respecter of democracy and national independence. Starting the American government on its subsequent policy of deficit spending.

Chief American Misperception: Not anticipating the fighting spirit of a great many Vietnamese.

Chief Sources: Browne (1965), Buttinger (1958), Fall (1964), Halberstam (1969). See also White (1968).

The SAC Alert of 1973

The Strategic Air Command's alerting of its nuclear forces at the end of the Arab–Israel War of 1973 is the least prominent of the 12 acts of force considered here, but it may well have started the long and tragic decline of détente between then and 1985.

At the end of the "Yom Kippur" War, Israel was winning. Henry Kissinger, as Secretary of State, wanted to retain rapport with both sides in order to make the kind of peace that he did proceed to make. He did not want Israel to win too decisively. He went to Moscow, and, together with Brezhnev, he hammered out a cease-fire agreement that gave Israel the victory without humiliating Egypt. It was then agreed to by both Golda Meir and Anwar Sadat.

General Sharon violated it. He wanted a decisive victory and continued to attack, surrounding the Egyptian Third Army on the east side of the Suez Canal and cutting it off from food and water. At that point, Brezhnev, apparently elated by his cooperation with Kissinger, proposed a further type of cooperation—that Soviet and American forces should enforce the cease fire on General Sharon, and he added that if this was not agreeable to the United States, the Soviet Union would be willing to do it alone. Apparently alarmed at the prospect of allowing any Soviet troops into the Middle East and the likelihood that he could not have a free hand to make peace in the way he wanted to, Kissinger, doubtless with President Nixon's approval, announced the SAC Alert. It worked. Brezhnev did not repeat his offer of cooperation or his "threat" of intervening unilaterally if the United States was not willing.

Good Results: Kissinger succeeded in keeping Soviet troops out of the Middle East and in gaining the free hand he wanted.

Bad Results: Kissinger may well have missed a fine opportunity to deepen the détente through continuing cooperation with the Soviet Union in the Middle East. He certainly puzzled and angered the Soviet leaders who could see no valid reason for inflicting such a humiliation on them. It may have been the first step in the long death of the détente of the early 1970s that began in 1973 and ended only with the coming of Gorbachev in 1985.

Chief American Misperception: Lack of empathy with the Russians.

Chief Sources: Sachar (1976).

The Persian Gulf War, 1990–1991

Saddam Hussein is a tough, ruthless, pitiless dictator. He has started two wars: one long one against Iran (1980–1988) and one short one against Kuwait (1990–1991). However, like many other acts of aggression, his were probably based predominately on fear. His attack on Iran stemmed mainly from a political kind of fear, whereas his attack on Kuwait stemmed mainly from an economic kind.

He can never forget that his is a divided country with his power base, the Sunnis, in the center, rebellious and hostile Kurds in the north, and in the south, Shiites, who share the religion that predominates across the border in Iran. He can never forget that his neighbor to the east is Iran, a country much larger and basically more powerful than his, and, after the Khomeini revolution of 1979, aggressively hostile to Saddam. Khomeini had declared openly his desire to unseat Saddam as too Western and too "atheist." Saddam's attack on Iran in 1980, therefore, was in large part a desire to preempt such an attack on him by Iran.

The war ended with Saddam almost bankrupt. He had hoped for financial support from the brother Arab countries that were richer in oil than Iraq was. Kuwait especially had been unwilling to join even though, from Iraq's standpoint, it was an Arab versus non-Arab war, and, in self-defense, they should have joined him in fighting it. Instead, they loaned him a large sum of money, which they could easily afford. He interpreted it as not a real loan but their (insufficient) contribution to the common Arab cause. The Kuwaitis were, in fact, extremely selfish and greedy.

They had some 220 billion dollars in investments and could easily afford to offer what Saddam desperately needed. His budget was geared to an oil price of about $18.00 a barrel. In large part because of Kuwait's undercutting the agreed on OPEC price, the market was glutted, and the price had gone down to $11.00. The economic danger to Iraq was heightened by Kuwait's demand for repayment of the large war debt.

There is a strong case for America's fighting and restoring Kuwait's independence. However, there is no case at all for its failure to promote a kind of negotiation that might have prevented the war.

Saddam had a number of legitimate grievances (Hilsman, 1992; Viorst, 1994). Kuwait refused to cancel the debt incurred by Iraq during the war with Iran, although it had actually agreed with Saddam that it was a common defense against a dangerously aggressive Iran. Kuwait had undercut the OPEC price of oil as indicated previously in a way that was disastrous for Iraq. It had engaged in slantwise drilling in the Rumaila oil field on their common border. It had refused to sell the mud flat small islands, Bubiyan and Warba, that were of no use to it but needed and wanted by Saddam to build a seaport on the Gulf. Kuwait had stubbornly refused to consider any of these grievances, and it had no comparable grievances against Saddam at that time.

Instead of refusing to take any position on this conflict, as U.S. Ambassador April Glaspie did, the United States could have appropriately brokered some compromise position that would have given each side what it wanted most, such as preserving Kuwait's territorial integrity and doing nothing about the oil prices but urging it to forgive Iraq's war debt, to stop the slantwise drilling and to sell two islands.

It did nothing of the sort; instead, there is much evidence now (Viorst, 1994) that American officials consistently assured Kuwait that America would fully back it up no matter what it did in the negotiations. This reinforced Kuwait's intransigence, and a war that was disastrous for Kuwait as well as Iraq occurred, although the kind of concessions made by the United States in both the Berlin Crisis and the Cuban Missile Crisis might perhaps have prevented it.

The story from then on is familiar and includes such a spectacular victory for the international community led by the United States that it does not need to be reviewed here. This is in striking contrast to what happened to the League of Nations and to the international community as a result of the League's failure to stop or punish Mussolini's invasion of Ethiopia.

A great many in the West have felt that the job was left unfinished because the international force did not invade Iraq, capture Saddam, and remove him from power. That is unfair. In seeking allies, Secretary Baker and President Bush had consistently stressed that the operation had only two purposes: to liberate Kuwait and to destroy most of Saddam's military power. There would surely have been far more American casualties and far greater international perception of the United States as an aggressor if it had unilaterally invaded and occupied Iraq.

What did happen was bad enough. The civilian infrastracture of Iraq was largely destroyed by America's air and missile power, which probably was unnecessary militarily. The embargo was continued and has survived until this writing. Both resulted in a catastrophe for the Iraqi people (Rouleau, 1995), and Saddam is still in power.

A major question is the following: What has been the effect of the war on the long-term relation between the Muslim world and the West? There is good reason to believe that, although most of the other Arabs look on Saddam as a cruel dictator, they see him also as a man who courageously stood up against western domination of the middle East and the Muslim world as a whole. This is a chief example of what Samuel Huntington (1993) calls "The Clash of Civilizations." It is possible that the Persian Gulf War has been second only to the Arab–Israeli conflict as a major cause of much worse violence in the future.

Good Results: Minimum cost in American lives. Protection of the oil fields and Israel. Showing that in this instance aggression did not pay, with some increased deterrence of aggression in the future. Survival of the United Nations as an effective instrument for peace.

Bad Results: Great loss of life by the Iraqis. Great economic cost to the Allied coalition, especially Turkey. Great and continuing suffering of the Iraqi people, which might have been prevented by America's urging appropriate concessions. Heightened Muslim ill will and, therefore, an increased "clash of civilizations."

Chief American Misperception: Lack of empathy with or sympathy for the Iraqi people and the Muslim world as a whole. Lack of empathy with Saddam's economic fear.

Chief Sources: Atkinson (1994), Baker (1995), Hilsman (1992), Miller (1990), Rouleau (1995), Viorst (1994).

The End of the War in Bosnia, 1995

It was fear—fear underlying hatred—that most powerfully motivated all three of the ethnic groups in Bosnia. The fear was not least among the Bosnian Serbs. On this, there is much agreement among writers on the subject (Djilas, 1993; Glenny, 1994; Malcolm, 1994; Owen, 1993; and see White, 1996), although some, notably Malcolm, attribute the fear largely to inflammatory propaganda by Milosevic.

What the Bosnian Serbs feared most was becoming a persecuted minority in the new Bosnian state set up (prematurely) in 1992. Their fear was not unfounded. During World War II, the Croats, playing Hitler's game, massacred hundreds of thousands of Bosnian Serbs. The Serb fear of the Muslims had much less basis in recent historical fact.

It is clear that the demonized image of Muslims in Bosnian Serb minds is much exaggerated, but this does not mean that their fear is less real. It is based on a truly diabolical image of both Croats and Muslims, and it is the main reason for their "offensive action" beginning in 1992.

What about the role of the United States, NATO, and the UN? It was ineffective and ignominious for more than 3 years. It became a terrible war with atrocities by all three of the ethnic groups and genocidal behavior on the part of the Serbs. There were over 2 million refugees. The UN was stymied by its own philosophy of neutrality and use of peace-keeping forces only to keep a peace on which both sides agreed. President Clinton probably could have played a constructive role without using force if he had strongly supported the Vance-Owen Peace Plan (Glenny, 1994), but he did not.

Finally, especially atrocious behavior by the Serbs, which occurred in the mainly Muslim city of Srebrenica, galvanized a willingness in both western Europe and the United States to intervene. NATO was now willing to exert decisive military force to obtain genuine negotiations and a political settlement. The air strike worked like a charm. There were genuine negotiations at Dayton, and a peace settlement was evolved, so fair that during the subsequent year and one half (this is being written in October, 1997) there have been virtually no American casualties and no organized warfare.

Good Results: A long and terrible war was ended. A settlement, probably much fairer than could have been achieved if the struggle between the groups had been allowed to take its natural course, was achieved. Respect for the international community and for its possible peacekeeping role was largely restored.

Bad Results: The massive NATO air strike undoubtedly cost lives, but the loss was probably minimal because the strike was concentrated on military targets.

Chief American Misperceptions: Not seeing the opportunity to nip the whole war in the bud by collective action immediately after the Serb shelling of Dubrovnic, based partly on nonempathy with the intensity of Serb fears.

Chief Sources: DeKleva (1955), Djilas (1993), Glenny (1994), West (1994); see also White (1996).

Lesser Interventions

There is a darker side to the picture of American interventions overseas. The focus of this article on the 12 judged to be most prominent has necessarily meant giving little attention to the much larger number of less prominent interventions, and it is my impression that the net long-term results of these lesser ones have been mainly bad from a humanist point of view. Blechman and Kaplan (1978) list 215 instances of American use or threat of force since 1945 and consider the results generally satisfactory. However, there are many instances in which, usually without using or explicitly threatening force, the United States has given moral, political, or economic support to military dictators or landowning oligarchies. In Chiang Kai-shek's China, in the Shah's Iran, in Batista's Cuba, in Somoza's Nicaragua, in Pinochet's Chile, in Angola and Zaire, in Guatemala, El Salvador, the Dominican Republic, and several other places, the basic pattern has been similar to that of Vietnam.

That has been unfortunate, to say the least, even from the standpoint of enlightened national self-interest. America's pretensions to be in favor of democracy everywhere look hollow and hypocritical in the eyes of most of the rest of the world. As Lebow and Stein (1995) have put it, American foreign policy has lost legitimacy.

The Nuclear Arms Race

Have nuclear weapons promoted peace? The proudest boast of the one-sided nuclear deterrers is that they have. They maintain that the strength of the American nuclear arsenal (some 10,000 warheads at its highest point) was the essential reason that World War III never occurred throughout the entire history of the Cold War; because of it, the Soviet Union did not dare either to start a nuclear war or to invade western Europe.

This proposition deserves careful consideration. Strictly speaking, it does not belong in this article; it is not one of our 12 examples of the use or threat of force. However, the possession of nuclear weapons is certainly an implied threat of terrible destruction, and the subject is too important a part of peace psychology to be wholly neglected here.

Among "national security" specialists, there is some agreement that the mere possession of a significant number of nuclear weapons on each side has been a powerful deterrent. That consensus is not disputed here. However, the argument of the nuclear deterrers is dubious on two accounts: The size of the American nuclear arsenal may have been far greater than was necessary for the purpose of deterrence, and the Soviet Union may never have wanted to invade western Europe in the first place.

Lebow and Stein (1995) argue that the 10,000 nuclear warheads of the United States were a tremendous "overdose" of nuclear medicine. They exacerbated the fears on both sides, notably in the case of the Cuban Missile crisis, and were quite unnecessary because a much more limited number (let's say 500 warheads, many of them relatively invulnerable on submarines or hardened missile sites) were quite sufficient for deterrent purposes.

The other argument is that the traumatic experience of World War II ensured that the Soviet Union would never have started any kind of big war in the first place. George Kennan (1972), perhaps the most widely known western specialist on the Soviet Union, maintains that, even at the very beginning, the Soviet Union expected to enlarge its power and influence through revolution rather than through military conquest. In effect, he argues that this is another case of *post hoc ergo propter hoc.*

The Soviet Union's unwillingness to invade western Europe coincided with their knowledge of the nuclear strength of the West, but that did not prove that its strength was the cause of there being no invasion. That hypothesis rests mainly on the dubious assumption that the Soviet Union wanted it in the first place, even at the cost of war.

The Cold War as a Whole, 1945–1989

The Cold War was a whole (a pattern, a *gestalt*, a system of mutually interacting parts) that was definitely more than the sum of its parts considered separately. Its core was the exaggerated fear on both sides that led to offensive actions by both.

If falls naturally into two parts. The first can be called the Stalin period (1945–1953) and the second the post-Stalin period. Most of the offensive actions by the Soviet Union were concentrated in the Stalin period, and the causal relation is direct. He was the absolute ruler of the Soviet Union from at least as early as 1929 until his death in 1953.

Stalin was an obsessive demonizer. His dominant defense mechanism was projection; he apparently could not bear to contemplate his numberless crimes or the natural reactions of others to them and had to project all of the blame on others, both domestic and foreign. There is a real analogy here to paranoid delusions of persecution, because psychiatrists generally see projection as the primary mechanism in paranoid psychoses.

He started the Cold War. Or rather, he reignited the conflict that had existed throughout the whole prewar period (1917–1941). He did it at a time when there was little or no provocation by the West. In 1945 and early 1946, most of the people in the West, although ambivalent, were friendly to the Soviet peoples, sincerely grateful for their major share in the defeat of Hitler, and certainly not harboring any aggressive designs against the Soviet Union. His demonizing was made almost out of whole cloth. It resulted in offensive behavior that had little basis in any similar offensive action by the West.

Soviet actions between 1945 and 1953 included (a) the takeover of most of eastern Europe, chiefly by simply leaving Soviet troops in the area and creating replicas of Stalin's communism using the troops as leverage; (b) leaving Soviet troops in northwestern Iran until almost forced to remove them by the UN; (c) rejecting the Baruch Plan for international control of nuclear weapons; (d) rejecting Marshall Plan aid; (e) trying to starve out the West Berliners in the first Berlin Crisis (1948–1949); (f) promotion of communism in the third world, especially Indonesia; and (g) approving Kim Il Sung's plan for attacking South Korea.

As indicated previously in discussing the deterrent value of the Korean War, after 1953, there was no comparable expansionist military action by the USSR. It backed down more than the United States did in the Berlin and Cuban crises; the crackdowns on Hungary and Czechoslovakia were within the Soviet sphere without crossing the dividing line; and the "invasion" of Afghanistan was motivated by strong defensive considerations. It was primarily an effort to keep a hitherto friendly nation from becoming an unfriendly one on the vulnerable southern border of the USSR (Garthoff, 1985; Kennan, 1980; Petrov, 1980; see also White, 1984).

Meanwhile, the United States had the record described earlier in this article. It is my personal view that the American role after 1953 has been somewhat more offensive than that of the USSR. If that is true, the United States has been demonizing its Soviet opponent and idealizing itself to a considerable degree.

Chief Sources: Acheson (1969), Gaddis (1992), Garthoff (1985), Hobsbawm (1994), Kennan (1972), Solzhenitsyn (1974–1978), Tucker (1990), Ulam (1971); see also White (1984).

MISPERCEPTION AS A REASON FOR BAD RESULTS

The problem of misperception in international affairs was first recognized by a large number of political scientists with the publication in 1976 of Robert Jervis's *Perception and Misperception in International Politics*. Richard Ned Lebow (1981) added description in some detail of misperception during international crises in *Between Peace and War: The Nature of International Crisis*. The work with greatest relevance to this study, however, was that of Jack Levy's (1983) "Misperception and the Causes of War: Theoretical Linkages and Analytical Problems." In this work, he presents a careful conceptualization and discussion of types of international misperception and the various ways in which they are related to war.

The six forms of misperception discussed and illustrated here are

- A demonized enemy image.
- An idealized self-image.
- Overconfidence.
- Underconfidence.
- Nonempathy with opponents.
- Nonempathy with intervening third parties. (See Table 2.)

A Demonized Enemy Image

The demonized enemy image (defined here as an exaggeration of the actual evil in an adversary's character) is with little doubt the most common concomitant of war and probably the most important direct cause of offensive action. It was prominent in each of the four American offensive actions that turned out most badly: the invasion of North Korea, the Bay of Pigs, the Vietnam War, and the SAC Alert of 1973. The overall demonized image of the rulers of the Soviet Union, which in

TABLE 2
Misperceptions Associated With Bad Results

Events	Demonized Enemy	Idealized Self	Over-confidence	Non-Empathy With	
				Opponents	Third Parties
Mainly good results					
World War II in Europe					
World War II in Asia					
Defense of South Korea		*		?	
Cuban Missile Crisis		*		?	
Berlin Crisis					
Bosnia War		? *		? *	
Mainly bad results					
Invasion of North Korea	?	*	*	*	*
Bay of Pigs	*	*		*	
Vietnam War	*	*		*	
Balanced good and bad results					
World War I	?			?	
Persian Gulf	?			*	*

Note: An asterix indicates presence to a significant degree of the misperception indicated at the head of the column.

retrospect was fully valid in the case of Stalin and Stalinism, became much less valid after his death. Yet, it continued with ups and downs until 1985. It was present and conspicuous in the first phase of the Berlin and Cuban Missile Crises. It diminished as President Kennedy became more familiar with the genuine fears of Nikita Khrushchev and with his wounded pride and rejection of the idea that the United States should keep its missiles in Turkey while demanding removal of Soviet missiles from Cuba.

Realistic empathy is the best antidote to devil images, and, in this case, the diminishing of Khrushchev's and Kennedy's devil images may have been necessary for the creative compromises that were worked out, which in turn may have been necessary for the resolution of the crises.

A similar and much more drastic diminishing of American devil images occurred in both Germany and Japan after the end of World War II. As we have seen, the friendliness of both to American troops occupying their countries was amazing. The reason may have been a contrast effect—the generalization that, although small changes are likely to be ignored, large changes tend to be exaggerated. The expectations of the Germans and the Japanese as to how they would be treated were surely influenced by government propaganda in both countries during the war, promising that, if they lost the war, the people would suffer a cruel fate at the hands of the American devils. Goebbel's "strategy of gloom" made this its central theme, and, in both countries, the extent and real cruelty of American fire bombing, not to mention atom bombing in Japan, gave a basis in reality for what the propaganda promised. When, in fact, the terms of peace and the treatment of the people by the Americans were friendly, rather than cruel, the surprise must have been great; and, if the contrast effect operated, it would have also been exaggerated. Devil images are especially dangerous to peace when the evil of the enemy is perceived as inherent and its hostility as changeless, implacable. The consequence is that one's own country makes no effort to change its hostility that is seen as unchangeable. That is conspicuously true, for instance, in the case of Arab and Israeli images of each other. In such a case, there may be no alternative to compulsion from outside to achieve a compromise that one side or the other would be sure to veto in the absence of compulsion.

Four lines of psychological thinking suggest reasons for the demonizing. The first, of course, is the projection mechanism. The second is the "dispositional" attribution described by Jones and Nisbett (1971). If an opponent's actions hurt the observer's nation in any way, they are almost sure to be seen as "bad" and to result in attributing badness to a supposed aggressive disposition of the opponent. The third is undue cognitive simplicity—the extreme of what Tetlock calls "cognitive simplicity" (Tetlock & McGuire, 1986). In several ways, Tetlock calls attention to the tendency of the lazy human mind to oversimplify an extremely complex world, and the Good Guys and Bad Guys image is an extreme form of unrealistic simplicity. The fourth is Heider's (1958) "balance" theory and the cases in which an actor and his actions are somehow merged, and it is assumed that a "bad" action must have been performed by a "bad" group or individual.

Idealization of the Self

Idealization of the self is defined here as the product of flattering self-deception through focusing on exaggerated real virtues plus rationalizing, projecting, denying, or simply ignoring any possible sins or defects of the national self. It is more basic than the diabolical enemy image in at least one way: In the projection mechanism, which is one main source of devil images, the original need is to escape blame. The formula is, "We are not to blame; they are."

It increases the likelihood of offensive action in several ways. First, it takes off the brakes of conscience that might otherwise keep a nation from engaging in such acts. In the words of Kurt Lewin (1951), the fear and power hunger of an aggressor would be called driving forces, whereas both conscience and fear of condemnation by other nations could be called restraining forces.

In the many documents that became available after World War I, representing what the Germans and Austrians were saying to each other during the crisis of 1914, it would be difficult to find any reference to aggression as possibly applying to either of the great offensive actions that were being considered. The attack on Serbia was "taking a firm stand." Germany's action was "loyally supporting our ally," it was "setting a dam to the Pan-Slav flood," it was "cleaning out the nest of assassins in Belgrade," and it was "teaching the Serbs a lesson they will never forget." The word *aggression* was not even used in the form of a question: Could their opponents possibly consider them aggressors? It was selective inattention (simply ignoring) on a large scale, along with rationalization and projection.

Second, the feeling of innocence made them unlikely to realize that other nations might see the same act (quite differently) as a crime. They considered, but belittled, the real possibility that France and Russia would take the attack on Serbia as an occasion for war. That the British in their moral outrage at the attack on Belgium and on France might come into the war was hardly considered at all by the Kaiser and Bethmann-Hollweg. That was a monumental mistake. The Kaiser and Bethmann-Hollweg, rather than admitting the mistake, became furious at Britain for "striking a man from behind while he was fighting for his life against two assailants." The coming in of the British may have lost the Germans the war; it had much to do with the later coming in of the Americans. Similarly, exhilarated by MacArthur's victory at Inchon and feeling that any action against Communists must be legitimate in the great conflict between freedom and Communism, the Americans had few thoughts about how that offensive action would be perceived by the Chinese.

Third, passivity and unwillingness to risk any losses may be rationalized as a virtue. We say, "We are sane and decent people. We believe in peace, unlike those quarrelsome foreigners." There was self-righteous complacency in the unwillingness of Americans to participate actively against Hitler from 1936 to 1941, in their unwillingness to do anything active against Japan from 1931 to 1941, and in their unwillingness to abandon a neutral position in Bosnia from 1942 to 1945.

Has the United States committed "sins" in its international behavior during the 20th century? That question calls urgently for a definition of sin in an international context. In that context, sin is defined here as behavior that, in the light of available evidence at the time, is likely to result in much harm from the standpoint of human welfare, enlightened national self-interest, or both.

Here is my very personal list of nominations:

1. America's role in the inequities of the Versailles Treaty.
2. Not joining the League of Nations.
3. Not accepting the French proposal that if the United States did not insist on repayment of war debts, France would not insist on reparations from Germany. We could have afforded that sacrifice. At that point, they could not.
4. Not taking the lead during the 1920s in a collective drastic revision of the Treaty of Versailles, along with Allied support for France against future German invasion.
5. In the 1930s, not insisting that Hitler use orderly and democratic methods in his effort to reunify the German people.

6. Not taking the lead in collective action to use force if necessary to keep him from taking over non-German land.
7. Our invasion of North Korea.
8. Many lesser interventions, on behalf of dictators or military oligarchies, in third world countries against popular movements that have often been Communist led.
9. The Bay of Pigs.
10. At the outset of the Cuban Missile Crisis, Kennedy's excessive commitment to a policy of no concessions, which he found difficult to modify publicly.
11. The Vietnam War.
12. A policy of one-sided support of Israel even after the Israelis began violating the spirit of UN Resolution 242 by clinging to all of the Sinai, the West Bank, and the Golan Heights.
13. The SAC Alert of 1973, which deeply antagonized the Soviets for no good reason.
14. Congress' rejection of the Salt 2 Treaty, which the Administration had finally managed to achieve.
15. Carter's many-sided over-reaction to the defensively motivated Soviet intervention in Afghanistan.
16. In the period following the end of Communism and the Cold War, not giving sufficient help to the desperately needful USSR.
17. The economic embargo of Cuba, which hurt the Cuban people without dislodging Castro.
18. The economic embargo of Iraq after the war ended, which continued to hurt the Iraqi people without dislodging Saddam Hussein.
19. The destruction of the civilian infrastructure of Iraq, which hurt the people greatly and was probably not necessary militarily.
20. Failure to get Kuwait to accept appropriate concessions that might have prevented the Persian Gulf War.

The "sinfulness" of many of these is controversial (but will not be defended in this article). Many are "sins" of omission not commission and, hence, are easy to forget. Many of them have probably been forgotten or never entered the conscious minds of most Americans at all. However, that is just the point. Selective inattention is a frequent sin, not only of the general public but also of educators and the mass media; they could have seriously considered the moral aspects and have not done so.

Overconfidence

Most of the initiators of offensive action that ended in defeat started with military overconfidence.

American instances of overconfidence—the invasion of North Korea, the Bay of Pigs, and Vietnam—have already been described. However, the phenomenon is so frequent that several examples of it in other nations should be quickly summarized here: The Germans initiated World War I and lost it; at the outset, General Moltke believed he could defeat France quickly before the British could intervene in enough force to prevent it; the Kaiser told his troops in August that they would be "home before the leaves fall."

Hitler lost his war against the USSR, although, at the outset, he had told others that the war would be "like a children's game in a sandbox" compared with the war he had just finished against Poland (as cited in Levy, 1989, p. 284).

The Serbs had good reason to believe that with the Yugoslav National Army (JNA) on their side and with the Muslims hardly prepared militarily at all they could quickly defeat at least the Muslims if not also the Croats.

Kim Il Sung was fatuously overconfident before attacking South Korea. He told Khrushchev that he was "certain" that he could win a quick victory (Khrushchev, 1970).

It is a striking fact that none, or almost none, of these instances of overconfidence has been based on a serious miscalculation of the power ratio between the initiator and its victims, using the tangible indicators of power on which Singer (1972) and Bueno de Mesquita (1981) have focused. All, or nearly all of them, have occurred because the initiator failed to estimate properly the psychological nature of their immediate victims or, more frequently, third parties.

Let us take first the frequent interventions by third parties. In World War I, the intervening third parties were Britain and, much later, the United States. In World War II, in Europe, the intervening parties were again Britain, which fought with quite unexpected tenacity, and the United States. In World War II, in Asia, the intervener was the United States. In Kim Il Sung's attack on South Korea, it was the United States. In the American intervention in North Korea, it was China. In the Berlin Crisis, it was the United States. In the Cuban Missile Crisis, it was the Soviet Union's intervention in the continuing conflict between the United States and Cuba. In the Persian Gulf War, it was the international community, especially the United States.

Instances of unexpected resistance by the victims themselves are less numerous but equally striking, notably the Bay of Pigs and the resistance to American intervention by many Vietnamese.

In a number of other 20th century conflicts, there has been a similar blindness to the likelihood of strong patriotic resistance. For instance, Hitler's miscalculation was based mainly on his extreme underestimate of the nationalist spirit of the Russians, who were defending their homeland against the German invaders. Another is the unexpected resistance of Israel to the concerted Arab attack in 1948.

It is evident that in all of these instances, there has been, in the minds of the war initiators, a self-defeating lack of real empathy with their immediate victims or more often with third parties who were potential interveners. It is this intangible psychological factor, not any crude miscalculation of tangible military factors, that has been largely responsible for the overconfidence that has often led to war.

Underconfidence (Worst-Case Thinking)

Underconfidence is surely a much less frequent reason for uses or threats of force than is overconfidence. It does not appear directly in any of our 12 case studies. It does occur, however, and, therefore, deserves attention.

A clear case of it is the "missile gap" that was not and, in the time just before the Berlin and Cuban Missile Crises, was unusually extreme because it soon appeared that there was a real missile gap, but in the opposite direction, favorable to the United States. It may be that American military men, and perhaps American intelligence, had a tendency to worst-case thinking when comparing American military strength with that of the Soviet Union. This has another root—a desire to gain larger appropriations from Congress, but it may also be quite genuine. In my observation, overanxious worst-case thinking may be at least as common in everyday affairs as overoptimistic wishful thinking. It may, in fact, often be a reaction to the temptation of wishful thinking; it feels more realistic to be pessimistic.

If and when worst-case thinking contributes to arms races, including nuclear arms races, it becomes a source of war, because such races, it has been well demonstrated, increase the danger of war, probably because they continually generate exaggerated fear and demonized enemy images. What about the years in which the United States was, according to our analysis, over reluctant to enter a war (the years 1936 to 1941 against Hitler, the years 1931 to 1941 against Japan, and the years 1991 to 1995 against the Serbs)? Is it likely that underconfidence played some part in that over reluctance? This seems somewhat unlikely in that the United States has always been one of the safest and, for many years in this century, one of the strongest countries in the world and has usually shown a complacent self-confidence in foreign affairs rather than underconfidence. Americans know they are strong and could fight well if they had to. It is more probable that the reluctance has been based on inertia, isolationism, general self-centeredness, and, in recent years, an obsessive fear of losing even one American life, rather than underconfidence.

Perhaps worst-case thinking adds most to the danger of mistaken offensive action when it reinforces a long-term fear of an adversary conceived as unchangeably, implacably hostile. There are a surprising number of cases in which short-term overconfidence has been combined with long-term underconfidence or excessive fear. One of them was German thinking at the outset of World War I. The Germans overestimated the danger of losing a war in 1917 or later when Russia would be supposedly much stronger, Britain perhaps more closely united with France and

Russia, and Austria–Hungary perhaps thoroughly broken into fragments. This fear, in the back of their minds, was combined with what was probably overconfidence that, in a conflict between them and the French alliance, they could quickly win in 1914. Even Hitler had a similar fear (Rich, 1973) of a long-term future in which the "Slavic hordes," then armed with western technology and weapons, would overwhelm the Germanic peoples, unless, in the meantime, the Slavic world could be greatly weakened.

Nonempathy With Opponents

Empathy is defined here not as sympathy but as simply understanding what is in the minds of others. This section will be devoted to an exploration and elaboration of four ways in which a lack of realistic empathy with others conflicts with enlightened national self-interest.

Lack of empathy has contributed to "bad" results in four ways: (a) underestimating the high-flown ambitions of an aggressor, (b) demonizing the enemy (ignoring the more "human" feelings such as fear), (c) underestimating the likelihood of third parties intervening, and (d) Underestimating the fighting spirit of a people who are defending their homeland.

Underestimating the high-flown ambitions of an aggressor.   This is Jervis's (1976) idea of the deterrence model in which a determined aggressor is unresponsive to conciliation and likely to interpret it as weakness. It fits well the two cases to which Jervis applied it: World War II in Europe and World War II in Asia. The United States and, in fact, the entire "international community," if it had existed, would have been wise if it had been militarily prepared and psychologically ready to be firm with Hitler from the very beginning of his forcible expansion in the Rhineland.

The story of how the West, as a whole, and especially Neville Chamberlain underestimated the extent of Hitler's ambition to expand in the East is now so well-known that it does not need to be summarized here. Less well recognized, however, is the similar story of the expansion of Japan on the Asian mainland beginning in 1895 and the slowness with which its intention to control all of the Far East was recognized by the rest of the world.

The United States's involvement in both these instances of nonempathy was conspicuous. It finally reached the point of willingness to join the war against Hitler more than 2 years after that war started, and it did not begin to fight Japan until more than 4 years after its all-out attack on China began in 1937.

This underestimation of real danger was not a reason for using or threatening to use force. Quite the contrary, it was a reason for failing to use force when it would have been wise to use it. However, it was in both cases so important that it insistently demands mention here. What was needed in both wars was not unilateral action by the United States but full and early participation by the United States in international action.

Demonizing the enemy.   As we have seen, the demonized enemy image is a basic cause of war, especially if it takes the form of "they are the aggressors; they are out to get us if we do not get them first." In this form, it can lead straight to preventive war or preemptive war.

The sovereign antidote to the demonized enemy image is realistic empathy. The moment we begin to try to put ourselves in the adversary's place and look through his eyes at his situation as he may perceive it we may begin to realize that he has understandable fears, understandable sources of anger (even at us), and probably a great desire for an acceptable kind of peace. These things are genuine if he is not a real devil like Hitler or Stalin but a human being more or less like us. Our characterization of him as having an evil, aggressive disposition fades as we begin to see his situation as he sees it. Our own outlook becomes more "situational" and less "dispositional" (Jones & Nisbett, 1971). Genuine negotiation then becomes possible as well as the making of concessions in which they are needed and feasible.

Empathy and the demonized enemy image are, as a rule, mutually exclusive. An image of the enemy as a monster precludes even beginning to think of him as a person, and trying to think of him as a person precludes thinking of him as a monster.

Thinking of him as a person includes recognizing his situation as you see it and also as he may see it. The latter is often especially difficult and unpleasant because it includes seeing his devil image of one's own nation—his fears of what it may do to his country in the future and his anger at what it has done to his country in the past or present; in addition, wondering about the kernels of truth that his devil image may contain.

Not seeing the devotion of others to the defense of their homeland.   The American intervention in Vietnam is a prime example. Americans did not put themselves in the place of the Vietnamese, who remembered their previous subjection to French colonialism and saw American intervention as a new foreign invasion of their country. The result was a kind of fierce, tenacious resistance to the American intruders that amazed the American military. Here was the great, rich, and technically advanced United States. There was the small, poor, and technically backward Vietnam. Yet, it sustained a bitter war for 10 years and ended as the victor.

The Bay of Pigs is somewhat similar but not clearly an example of a people defending itself. The immediate and efficient capture of the Cuban interveners tells us little or nothing about the attitudes of the Cuban people. Other evidence, however, indicates that, at that time, a large majority of the Cuban people favored

Castro, which would have made an extension of intervention very difficult. Kennedy was surely right not to favor such an extension that could easily have become "another Hungary," in which America would appear, in the eyes of the world, as an actual aggressor putting down a patriotic and angry Cuban people.

These are the only examples of what might be called the "defense of homeland model" in our list of 12 instances of American acts of force, but many other offensive actions in the 20th century have run into the same great obstacle. The Germans, in 1914, probably did not expect the kind of tenacious patriotic resistance they encountered from the French, most of all at Verdun. Hitler probably did not foresee the effectiveness of the British air force at the time of the Battle of Britain as well as the tenacity of the British people under the rain of rockets that he sent. He surely underestimated enormously the fierceness and tenacity of the Russian opposition to his invasion. Probably, he took at face value the poor showing of the Russian troops in their previous attack on Finland, but that was psychologically different. In that case, the Russians were attacking, and the Finns were defending.

The Japanese did expect America to fight if they attacked at Pearl Harbor, but they did not expect the tenacity of purpose that America showed from then on. Like others, they had the idea that Americans were "soft." (Toland, 1970)

In 1945, the French began to try to reconquer the newly independent and proud state of Vietnam, but the Vietnamese showed the same dogged courage they later showed in what we call the Vietnam War. They showed it against the French for 9 years and against the Americans for another 10 years. What a people the Vietnamese are!

In 1948, at the beginning of their war of independence, the infant state of Israel faced a far larger number of embattled Arabs, who probably expected victory. However, the Israelis showed the fierce courage, organization, unity, leadership, and audacity that carried them through to victory.

In the 1950s, the Algerians, who were not militarily a match for the French, outlasted them. In the Iran–Iraq war, Saddam Hussein expected an Iran disorganized by the very recent Khomeni revolution. His attack actually united the Iranians enough to result in his being pushed back to where he started.

In 1995, the Russians, with their vast territory and far greater population, probably assumed that they could easily reincorporate their little province of Chechnya. They were wrong.

Underestimating the likelihood of third parties intervening.   When American leaders in 1950 decided to invade North Korea, they did not empathize enough with China's fear of having a strong and hostile power just across the Yalu River from Manchuria. MacArthur felt sure they would not dare to intervene. They did intervene with disastrous results for the United States.

That is the only one of our 12 cases in which the United States has made this particular error, but it has been made by other countries no less than nine times in the conflicts we have been describing:

- In 1914, the Germans and Austrians thought that Russia would probably not intervene on behalf of Serbia. It did.
- In 1914, the Germans did not expect Britain to intervene on behalf of Belgium and France. It did.
- When Hitler attacked Poland, he did not expect Britain to fight tenaciously or America to fight at all. They did.
- When Japan attacked China in 1937, it probably did not expect America to intervene. It eventually did.
- When Kim Il Sung told Stalin about his plan to attack South Korea, he also told him that he was sure he would win quickly. He did not.
- When the CIA and the Pentagon planned the invasion of Cuba at the Bay of Pigs, they half expected that a large number of the Cuban people would rise against Castro. They did not.
- When Khrushchev tried hard to absorb West Berlin, he probably did not expect the United States to protest effectively. It did.
- When Saddam Hussein grabbed Kuwait, he probably did not expect the United States to intervene with full force. It did.
- When the Serbs took 70% of the land of Bosnia, instead of the 50% they could plausibly claim, they probably did not expect NATO to intervene. It finally did.

It should be noted that, in all of these nine instances, the initiator of the offensive action lost what it set out to gain.

What were the thoughts and feelings in the mind of intervening government decision makers that were not recognized by the initiator of the offensive action? What did the initiator fail to empathize with when he engaged in such a self-defeating action? We Americans should have a ready answer because America was the intervener or one of the interveners in seven of these instances.

A political scientist or historian would be sure to supply a ready answer: the balance of power motive. In several of them that makes good sense. The British had a tradition of intervening in continental European wars in order to keep a balance of power on the continent that would never endanger Britain itself. In addition, to some extent, the United States has undertaken this role as "balancer."

In World War I, World War II in Europe, and World War II in Asia, or at least in the first two of them, that makes good sense. However, was the United States really so concerned with the balance of power in east Asia that it intervened between Japan and China for that reason? How about the Korean and Persian Gulf Wars, in which no great powers were involved and no collapse of the world balance seemed a possibility? Some supplementary motives should at least be considered.

Looking at what our own political leaders have said to the public when favoring one of these interventions, we find a large amount of moral indignation at the "war makers" as such. It is felt to be outrageous that in a century in which nations have nearly all learned the horrors of modern war, anyone should deliberately start another. The aggression should be countered and, if possible, punished. This is something other than the balance of power, and it is not necessarily the same as sympathy for an endangered underdog. It can be combined with the more modern idea that aggression should never be rewarded in any way. We have then four possibilities: a balance of power motive, indignation, sympathy, and deterrence. The reader can judge.

Why do the initiators of offensive action so often ignore or underestimate the danger that there will be intervention against what they are about to do? One answer seems obvious—nations are self-centered. They get wrapped up in their own concerns and tend to think only vaguely about how others perceive their behavior. Another answer is less obvious. It is that having rationalized what they are doing as obviously necessary, often for reasons of long-term self-defense, they tend to assume vaguely that this rationale is obvious to others also. That is seldom true. More often, others, if they are in any way rivals of the initiator, are likely to put the worst interpretation on any offensive action. They see the action but not its psychological context in the minds of the initiators. They forget that in others' minds, as in their own, devil images and exaggeration of the evil in others' actions are omnipresent.

It becomes clear that lack of realistic empathy underlies at least three of the four other misperceptions emphasized here. It underlies the demonized enemy image in that good or such natural human motives as fear are seldom attributed to the enemy—only power-hunger or greed. It underlies the idealized self-image in that the opponent's picture of one's own country, if understood, would raise disturbing questions about the morality or wisdom of what one is doing. It underlies overconfidence in that two major reasons for losing the war, other than relative weakness at the outset, are likely to be ignored: the fighting spirit of the victims in defense of their homeland and the motives of third parties who intervene successfully, such as the balance of power motive.

Underconfidence is the only one of the four that does not appear to have lack of realistic empathy as a main source.

SOME GUIDELINES

Do not demonize other peoples. Think of them first as human beings with needs somewhat like your own. Listen hard (although sceptically) to what they say about the situation they are in.

Imagine how you would feel and act if you were in their situation.

Do not idealize a state that has engaged in any offensive action. Consider early international use of force to stop it before it becomes too strong and confident.

If the international community has clear military superiority and is going to act anyway, it should act decisively. That is how to save lives.

Consider international use of force to end a disastrous war and make genuine negotiation possible.

Do not underestimate the fighting spirit of a people that believes it is fighting to defend its homeland.

Do not underestimate the balance-of-power motivation of a third state that may intervene on behalf of your opponent.

If you win decisively, be magnanimous with your defeated opponent. If possible, grant it much of what it wants most.

"Don't kick a guy when he's down." Punitive embargoes are usually both cruel and futile.

In a war-risking crisis, think creatively about a settlement that might give each party most of what it wants most.

Do not arm any more than necessary to get adequate deterrence.

Do not take any of these suggestions as true without exception. New situations will almost always differ in important ways from the ones described here.

REFERENCES

Acheson, D. (1969). *Present at the Creation*. New York: Norton.

Albertini, L. (1952–1957). *The Origins of the War of 1914* (Vol. 1–3). London: Oxford University Press.

Allison, G. (1971). *Essence of decision: Explaining the Cuban missile crisis*. Boston: Little, Brown.

Atkinson, R. (1994). *Crusade: The untold story of the Persian Gulf War*. Boston: Houghton Mifflin.

Baker, J. A., III. (1995). *The politics of diplomacy: Revolution, war, and peace, 1989–1992*. New York: Putnam.

Beschloss, M. R. (1991). *The crisis years*. New York: HarperCollins.

Blechman, V., & Kaplan, S. (1978). *Force without war: U.S. armed forces as a political instrument*. Washington, DC: The Brookings Institution.

Blight, J. G., Allyn, B. J., & Welch, D. A. (1993). *Cuba on the brink*. New York: Pantheon.

Browne, M. (1965). *The new face of war*. Indianapolis: Bobbs-Merrill.

Bueno de Mesquita, B. (1981). *The war trap*. New Haven, CT: Yale University Press.

Buttinger, J. (1958). *The smaller dragon*. New York: Praeger.

Cantril, H. (1967). *The human dimension: Experiences in policy research*. New Brunswick, NJ: Rutgers University Press.

DeKleva, K. (1955, July). *Psychiatry and genocide: The case of Dr. Karadzic*. Paper presented at the 18th meeting of the International Society of Political Psychology, Washington, DC.

Deutsch, M. (1986). The malignant (spiral) process of hostile interaction. In R. K. White (Ed.), *Psychology and the prevention of nucelar war* (pp. 131–156). New York: New York University Press.

Djilas, A. (1993). A profile of Slobodan Milosevic. *Foreign Affairs, 72*(3), 81–96.

Fall, B. B. (1964). *The two vietnams* (Rev. ed.). New York: Praeger.

Fay, S. B. (1966). *The origins of the World War* (Vol. 1 & 2). New York: Free Press. (Original work published 1928 & 1930)

Fischer, F. (1967). *Germany's aims in the first World War*. New York: Norton. (Original work published 1961)

Fulbright, J. W. (1966, May 15). "The fatal arrogance of power". *New York Times Magazine*.

Gaddis, J. (1992). *United States and the end of the cold war*. New York: Oxford University Press.

Garthoff, R. L. (1985). *Détente and confrontation*. Washington, DC: Brookings Institution.

George, A., & Smoke, R. (1974). *Deterrence in american foreign policy: Theory and practice*. New York: Columbia University Press.

Glenny, M. (1994). *The fall of Yugoslavia*. New York: Penguin.

Halberstam, D. (1969). *The best and the brightest*. New York: Random House.

Heiden, K. (1944). *Der Fuehrer*. Boston: Houghton Mifflin.

Heider, F. (1958). *The psychology of interpersonal relations*. New York: Wiley.

Hilsman, R. (1992). *George Bush vs Saddam Hussein: Military success! political failure?* Novato, CA: Lyford Books.

Hitler, A. (1943). *Mein Kampf*. Cambridge, MA: Houghton Mifflin, Riverside Press. (Original work published 1925 & 1927)

Hobsbawm, E. (1994). *The age of extremes: A history of the world, 1914–1991*. New York: Pantheon.

Huntington, S. P. (1993, Summer). The clash of civilizations. *Foreign Affairs, 72*, 22–49.

Jervis, R. (1976). *Perception and misperception in international politics*. Princeton, NJ: Princeton University Press.

Jones, E., & Nisbett, R. (1971). *The actor and the observer: Divergent perceptions of the causes of behavior*. Morristown, NJ: General Learning Press.

Kagan, D. (1995). *On the origins of war and the preservation of peace*. New York: Doubleday.

Kennan, G. F. (1972). *Memoirs* (Vol. 2). Boston: Little, Brown.

Kennan, G. F. (1980, April). Imprudent response to the Afghanistan crisis? *Bulletin of the Atomic Scientists*, pp. 7–9.

Keynes, J. (1921). *The economic consequences of the peace*. New York: Harper & Row.

Khrushchev, N. (1970). *Khrushchev remembers*. Boston: Little, Brown.

Lebow, R. N. (1981). *Between peace and war: The Nature of International Crisis*. Baltimore: Johns Hopkins Press.

Lebow, R. N., & Stein, J. (1995). *We all lost the cold war*. Baltimore: Johns Hopkins Press.

Levy, J. S. (1983). Misperception and the causes of war: Theoretical linkages and analytical problems. *World Politics, 36*, 75–99.

Levy, J. S. (1989). The causes of war: A review of theories and evidence. In P. E. Tetlock, J. L. Husbands, R. Jervis, P. C. Stern, & C. Tilly (Eds.), *Behavior, society, and nuclear war* (Vol. 1, pp. 209–333). New York: Oxford University Press.

Lewin, K. (1951). *Field theory in social science*. New York: Harper.

Malcolm, N. (1994). *Bosnia: A short history*. New York: New York University Press.

Miller, J. (1990). *Saddam Hussein and the crisis in the Gulf*. New York: Random House.

Morgenthau, H. (1967). *Politics among nations: The struggle for power and peace* (4th ed.). New York: Knopf.

Owen, D. (1993). The future of the Balkans, an interview. *Foreign Affairs, 72*(2), 1–9.

Petrov, V. (1980). New dimensions of soviet foreign policy. In F. D. Margiotta (Ed.), *Evolving strategic realties: Implications for U.S. policymakers* (pp. 16–38). Washington, DC: National Defense University Press.

Rich, N. (1973). *Hitler's war aims: Vol. I. Ideology, the Nazi State, and the course of expansion*. New York: Norton.

Rouleau, E. (1995, January/February). America's unyielding policy toward Iraq. *Foreign Affairs, 74*, 59–72.

Sachar, H. M. (1976). *A history of Israel: From the rise of Zionism to our time*. New York: Knopf.

Schmitt, B. (1958). *The coming of the war, 1914*. New York: Fertig.

Shirer, W. (1941). *Berlin Diary: The Journal of a Foreign Correspondent*. Boston: Little, Brown.

Shulman, M. D. (1965). *Stalin's Foreign Policy Reappraised*. New York: Atheneum. (Original work published 1963)

Singer, J. D. (1972). 'The correlates of war' project: Interim report and rationale. *World Politics, 24,* 243–270.

Smith, H. K. (1942). *Last train from berlin.* New York: Knopf.

Smith, W. S. (1987). *The closest of enemies.* New York: Norton.

Solzhenitsyn, A. (1974–1978). *Gulag Archipelago, 1818–1956* (Vol. 1, 2, & 3). New York: Harper & Row.

Taylor, A. J. P. (1961). *The origins of the second World War* (2nd ed.). New York: Fawcett, Atheneum.

Tetlock, P. E., & McGuire, C. B., Jr. (1986). Cognitive Perspective and Foreign Policy. In R. K. White (Ed.), *Psychology and the prevention of nuclear war* (pp. 255–273). New York: New York University Press.

Toland, J. (1970). *The rising sun; the decline and fall of the Japanese empire, 1936–1945.* New York: Random House.

Tuchman, B. (1962). *The guns of August.* New York: Macmillan.

Tuchman, B. (1970). *Stillwell and the American experience in China, 1911–1945.* New York: Macmillan.

Tuchman, B. (1984). *The march of folly: From Troy to Vietnam.* New York: Knopf.

Tucker, R. C. (1990). *Stalin in power.* New York: Norton.

Ulam, A. B. (1971). *The rivals: America and Russia since World War II.* New York: Viking.

Viorst, M. (1994). *Sandcastles.* New York: Knopf.

West, R. (1994). *Tito: And the rise and fall of Yugoslavia.* New York: Carroll & Graf.

White, R. K. (1949, April). Hitler, Roosevelt and the nature of war propaganda. *Journal of Abnormal and Social Psychology, 44,* 157–174.

White, R. K. (1968). *Nobody wanted war: Misperception in Vietnam and other wars.* New York: Doubleday.

White, R. K. (1984). *Fearful warriors: A psychological profile of U.S.–Soviet relations.* New York: Free Press.

White, R. K. (1996). 'Socialism' and 'capitalism': An international misunderstanding. *Foreign Affairs, 44,* 216–228.

White, R. K. (1996). Why the Serbs fought: Motives and misperceptions. *Peace and Conflict, 2,* 109–128.

Whiting, A. (1960). *China crosses the Yalu; the decision to enter the Korean War.* New York: Macmillan.

Wolfers, A. (1940). *Britain and France between two wars: Conflicting strategies of peace since Versailles.* New York: Harcourt, Brace.

PEACE AND CONFLICT: JOURNAL OF PEACE PSYCHOLOGY, 4(2), 129–136

Misperception and the Use of Force: A Commentary on Ralph White's "American Acts of Force"

Jack S. Levy

Rutgers University

Ralph White's argument about the important role of demonized enemy images, lack of realistic empathy, and misperception in the processes leading to crisis and war find important parallels in the theoretical and empirical literature on international relations. I emphasize that military superiority is not sufficient to deter adversary aggression and that White's proposed guidelines for policymakers have some overlap with contemporary theories of crisis management.

I feel honored to have this opportunity to write a commentary on Ralph White's essay, "American Acts of Force: Results and Misperceptions." This essay continues to develop and apply certain important themes that I first encountered when I read White's (1968) *Nobody Wanted War* as a graduate student. That book, along with some of his later work (White, 1984, 1986), helped to influence my own thinking and that of the international relations field more generally about the role of misperceptions in international conflict.[1] It is, thus, with considerable admiration for Ralph White that I approach this task of writing a scholarly commentary on his most recent essay.

The task of examining a dozen acts of force undertaken by the United States, evaluating their outcomes in terms of a number of criteria, explaining these actions and their consequences in terms of psychological and political variables, and proposing guidelines for future policy is, needless to say, an ambitious task. It may be too ambitious for an article-length study. One cannot expect the author, in a single

---

Requests for reprints should be sent to Jack S. Levy, Department of Political Science, 89 George Street, Rutgers University, New Brunswick, NJ 08901–1411.

[1]I recently came across a striking indicator of White's general influence: The *Social Science Citation Index* (1997) shows that, in 1996, other scholars cited White's work from the 1950s, 1960s, 1970s, 1980s, and 1990s. In an area known for the rather short half-life of its scholarship, this is remarkable.

article, to elucidate and defend his criteria of evaluation, justify his selection of cases, define all of his variables, support all his historical judgments, defend his explanations against alternative interpretations, and offer guidance for future policy.

For this reason, a comprehensive critical review of White's article that focused on case selection, research design, operationalization of key indicators, and normative criteria of evaluation would not be appropriate. As a political scientist, I think I can make more of a contribution by suggesting how some of White's arguments relate to the theoretical and empirical literature in international relations. In that literature, we will find added support for some of White's more general theoretical propositions, less support for others, and important linkages between some of White's explanatory concepts and other lines of theoretical argument by international relations theorists.[2]

Let me begin, however, with some quibbles that I have about White's assessments of the outcomes of a few cases and the criteria by which he evaluates them. Although I sympathize with the normative considerations underlying White's internationalist criteria, I think that the inclusion of a measure of the extent to which the use of force advances the national interest of the state would be appropriate, as any policy prescriptions must ultimately be made in terms of national interests, however broadly defined if they are to be effective.

White does this indirectly to a certain extent within his broadened category of military success, but I prefer that the political outcome be given more prominence, following von Clausewitz's (1976) conceptualization of war (and the use of force short of war) as an instrument of policy in pursuit of state interests. White raises a good point, however, when he argues that, if one abandons myopic short-term thinking and adopts longer term time horizons, the differences between his internationalist criteria and criteria based on "enlightened national self-interest" begin to vanish.

Disputes over specific criteria aside, however, I think that many readers will conclude in the end that White's classification of his 12 cases in terms of "good," "bad," and ambiguous results are fairly reasonable. The two that I take exception to are White's two "ambiguous" cases, World War I and the 1990–1991 Persian Gulf War. One can argue about the allies' wisdom in imposing a Carthaginian peace on Germany after the First World War, but the war's outcome of avoiding German hegemony on the continent clearly outweighed the costs of the war, and the American impact on that outcome was significant.[3]

---

[2]For reviews of the international relations literature on the causes of war, see Vasquez (1993) and Levy (1998).

[3]Recent research supports the argument for attributing primary responsibility to the war to Germany (Albertini, 1980; Fischer, 1961, 1975). In addition, perceptions of innocence by the German people after the war was strongly influenced by an extensive propaganda campaign by the German government (Herwig, 1987).

Debate continues as to whether the Bush Administration ended the Persian Gulf War prematurely. Given what we know now about Iraq's nuclear, chemical, and biological weapons programs and determination to develop them more fully, however, it is clear to me that the outcome of the war was positive in terms of White's internationalist criteria—certainly in comparison with a negotiated peace that left Iraq's weapons of mass destruction untouched and free from external monitoring.

White's general argument that, because of lack of empathy and misperceptions, states frequently do not do enough to avoid crises and wars commands greater support in some of his cases than he acknowledges in this essay. Although the American victory over Japan in the Pacific War was an unqualified success, one can certainly raise the question of whether the United States did everything possible to avoid the war. The United States oil embargo against Japan was a highly coercive policy that backed Japan into a corner and led its leaders to perceive no choice but to gamble on a war that they did not expect to win but that they hoped might force the United States into a negotiated settlement. In the end, however, I think it would have been difficult to find a negotiated compromise that would have satisfied both Roosevelt and the Japanese military leadership (Iriye, 1986).

Although many historians would agree with White's assessment that, after 1953, it was the United States who was the more aggressive of the two adversaries, White misses a chance in the earlier period to reinforce his argument regarding the importance of misperceptions in generating escalating conflict spirals. He goes too far in attributing responsibility for the origins of the Cold War to Stalin. White's statement that "there was little or no provocation by the West" is hard to reconcile with the United States' cutoff of lend–lease and denial of a loan to the Soviet Union, with Soviet perceptions of American atomic diplomacy in its use of the bomb against Japan, and its more general concerns about United States economic imperialism and "capitalist encirclement."

Having made these comments about some of White's specific historical cases, let me now turn to some respects in which White's analysis relates to the larger international relations literature on the use of force and the causes of war. I begin with the relation between misperception and war, for White's (1968) earlier work on this subject had a clear influence on the substantial international relations literature on misperception and war (Jervis, 1976, 1988; Lebow, 1981).

I agree entirely with White's assessment of the importance of a demonized enemy image, an idealized self image, absence of realistic empathy, overconfidence, and underconfidence in the processes leading to war. I differ from White only in that I would conceptualize the first three of these as the sources of misperceptions rather than as misperceptions per se. I would also emphasize that, under some conditions, misperceptions contribute to peace rather than to war, though through different causal paths. We also need to acknowledge that the concept of misperception involves some difficult problems of definition and measurement (Jervis, 1976, 1988; Levy, 1983).

There are a variety of types of misperceptions, but the ones most likely to have a major impact on the processes leading to war are misperceptions of the capabilities and intentions of adversaries and third states. Misperceptions of intentions may derive from secondary misperceptions of the adversary's (or third state's) value structure, its definition of its vital interests, its definition of the situation, its expectations about the future, and the domestic or bureaucratic constraints on its freedom of action (Levy, 1983). These, in turn, relate to White's concepts of demonized enemy images, absence of realistic empathy, idealized self-images, and other variables. Overconfidence in war results from underestimation of the adversary's capabilities relative to one's own and from misperceptions of both the intentions and capabilities of third states. Motivated biases and unmotivated distortions in information processing also affect these processes.[4]

Let me now turn to some of White's ideas on the use of force and relate them to research projects in the international relations literature on conventional deterrence, coercive diplomacy, and crisis management. In noting that most uses or threats of force by the United States (at least those in his sample) ended in military success, White emphasizes that each of these successes involved the defensive use of force to protect others and that each of the failures involved the aggressive use of force against others (as White defines the terms). We need to be careful in generalizing from White's analysis of 12 U.S. cases to international behavior more generally, however, even if we were to accept White's operationalizations of aggressive or defensive and success or failure and his evaluations in the U.S. cases.

There have been few systematic studies of this question in the literature, and studies that have been done focus on "initiation" rather than "aggression" because of the difficult problems involved in defining aggression. One study of wars involving great powers shows that initiators won only slightly more than one half the time in the 16th, 17th, and 18th centuries but were nearly twice as likely to win as targets were in the next two centuries (Wang & Ray, 1994). Because some initiators in fact fit White's category of "defender" (Israel in the 1967 war, for example), however, it is hard to directly compare this and related studies (Bueno de Mesquita, 1981; Maoz, 1983) with White's. The discrepancy between White's findings and those of others suggests, however, that further research on this question is necessary before we can generalize from White's findings.

Regardless of the exact proportion of aggressors that win or lose, White makes a strong argument that, in cases in which aggressors do lose, it is often the aggressor's lack of empathy with its adversary or with third parties that plays a

---

[4]Although there is some value in White's concept of a demonized enemy image, which he defines as exaggerations of evil in an adversary's character, we must be careful to distinguish this from more general perceptions of hostility in the game of *realpolitik*. President Kennedy perceived Khrushchev as a hostile adversary, but he did not, contrary to White, demonize Khrushchev or the Soviet people.

central role in its initiation of the use of force (see also White, 1968). The frequent inability of a state to understand how its adversary (or its adversary's allies) defines its national interest or perceives threats to those interests can lead to war or an escalation of war because (a) the threat or use of force provokes the adversary into escalating the crisis rather than coercing him into submission; (b) war, and sometimes even the threat of war, unites the adversary's warring parties at home and mobilizes the population for warfare to the extent that the aggressor failed to anticipate; and (c) the consequent miscalculation of third state intentions leads to a larger war than was anticipated. The conflict spiral in the 1967 Arab–Israeli war illustrates the first point. The Iraqi invasion of Iran in 1980 illustrates the second point, in that Sunnis in Iran supported the Shiite Iranian regime rather than the Sunni regime of the Iraqi invaders. The United States' war with China provides a classic example of the third point.

The importance of the absence of empathy that leads to misperceptions is related to White's argument that, although most cases of failed aggressive military action sprang from military overconfidence, almost all such cases involved not a miscalculation of tangible indicators of military power or military overconfidence but rather a faulty assessment of the "psychological nature" of their adversaries or third parties.

I would define "psychological nature" more broadly to include perceptions of the adversary's resolve, its intentions, its ability to mobilize its population for war, and the willingness of third parties to intervene in support of the adversary. Although there have been no systematic studies that compare the relative frequency of misperceptions of relative capabilities as opposed to misperceptions of intentions, White's argument derives some indirect support from both qualitative and quantitative studies of deterrence success and failure and of the effectiveness of military threats more generally (Levy, 1988).

These studies show that the relative balance of military capabilities—defined in terms of tangible indicators of power—do not always determine the outcome of international crises in terms of who prevails and who is forced to yield. A balance of military capabilities is not sufficient for either deterring the adversary from initiating military threats or from following through on those threats. In addition, the overall balance of power between states has at most a secondary impact on the success or failure of deterrence.

When states attempt to deter a potential aggressor from attacking a client state, however, there is evidence that the balance of conventional capabilities in proximity to the target does play an important role (Huth, 1988). Taken together, these findings are consistent with the argument that the utility of military threats depends on the threatener's possession of a spectrum of military capabilities and options appropriate to the level of the threat and the behavior that it is attempting to influence (George & Smoke, 1974). This point should be incorporated into White's guidelines for future policy.

The finding that superior military capabilities are not always sufficient for deterrence can be explained in part by the tremendous importance of the interests and resolve of the contending parties. George and Smoke (1974) emphasize that the "asymmetry of motivation" often has a greater impact than does the balance of power on crisis bargaining and outcomes, a finding that is supported in quantitative studies of all militarized disputes since 1815 (Bueno de Mesquita, 1981; Maoz, 1983). For this reason, it is clear that the absence of empathy that leads to misperceptions of the intentions and underestimation of the resolve of adversaries and their potential allies can play a significant role in the origins of international crises and wars.

I should mention two other factors that are important in explaining the offensive use of force. One, neglected by White, is the role of domestic political considerations. Under some conditions, political leaders beset with internal political and economic problems may be tempted to use military force beyond their borders. This might serve the purpose of securing external resources to help alleviate internal problems, which was the primary factor driving Saddam Hussein's invasion of Kuwait in 1990 (Freedman & Karsh, 1993). It might also serve as a means of diverting attention from internal problems and creating a "rally 'round the flag" effect to bolster political leaders' internal support, as illustrated by the Argentine invasion of the Malvinas in 1982 (Levy, 1989). Thus, domestic factors may play an important role in aggressive external action and may strongly reinforce political leaders' resolve not to back down in international crises.

Another factor that can affect states' resolve and intentions—one that White neglects in this study but that he has discussed elsewhere—is loss aversion. This theoretical concept derives from prospect theory and from the behavioral decision theory literature more generally. The basic argument is that people frame their choices around a reference point, overweight losses from that reference point relative to equivalent gains, and make risk-averse choices among gains but risk-acceptant choices among losses. They also adjust to gains much more quickly than to losses and, thus, reframe around new acquisitions but not around recent losses (Kahneman & Tversky, 1979).

The phenomena of loss aversion and the asymmetry of risk orientation for gains and losses has potentially important implications for state behavior in international crises and in international behavior more generally, although the problems involved in generalizing from controlled experimental studies to the ill-structured world of international relations are quite substantial (Levy, 1996, 1997).

One implication is that state leaders take more risks to maintain their international positions, reputations, and domestic political support than they do to enhance those positions. Moreover, after suffering losses (in territory, reputation, domestic political support, etc.), political leaders take excessive risks (relative to expected value calculations) to recover them, whereas, after making gains, political leaders reframe their reference points and take excessive risks to defend them against subsequent losses. Thus, if State A loses territory to State B, A will take excessive risks to maintain her gains, whereas B will take extreme risks to recover her losses.

Finally, there is an interesting overlap between White's guidelines for policy-makers and the guidelines for effective crisis management that some international relations theorists have developed. George (1989), for example, argues that certain "political requirements" of crisis management (limiting both one's political objectives in crisis and the means one employs) are necessary but not sufficient for resolving a crisis in a way that achieves the twin objectives of avoiding war without sacrificing vital national interests.

Statesmen must also adhere to a number of "operational requirements" of crisis management. These include (a) maintaining top-level civilian control of military options (rather than delegating politically-relevant decisions on the use of force to the military); (b) coordinating diplomatic and military moves in a combined politico–military strategy; (c) selecting military actions appropriate to limited crisis objectives; (d) selecting military actions (coupled with diplomatic signals) that demonstrate one's intentions to negotiate, while avoiding those actions that give the opponent the impression that one seeks a military solution, which might give the opponent the incentive to preempt; (e) creating pauses in the tempo of military actions to slow down momentum of events and minimize the danger of loss of control; and (f) selecting diplomatic and military options that provide the opponent a face-saving compromise (for reasons of domestic politics as well as international reputation) that leaves her a way out of the crisis that is compatible with her fundamental interests.

CONCLUSION

I have tried to show that, in his article on "American Acts of Force," Ralph White has identified a number of patterns and suggested several explanations that have some important parallels in the theoretical and empirical literature on international relations. This is perhaps not surprising, for some of that literature reflects the influence of some of White's earlier work over a period of three decades.

Not all readers will agree with White's criteria for the evaluation of the use of force, and some will quibble with certain aspects of his methodology, his explanations for certain patterns and particular outcomes, or his guidelines for policymakers. It is clear, however, that White's essay reflects a strong commitment to an internationalist perspective and to the important role of the scholar in identifying patterns in world politics, grounding those patterns in concrete historical cases, and generating policy-relevant theories that will be useful to policymakers as well as to scholars.

REFERENCES

Albertini, L. (1980). *The origins of the war of 1914* (Vols. 1–3; I. M. Massey, Trans.). Westport, CT: Greenwood.

Bueno de Mesquita, B. (1981). *The war trap.* New Haven, CT: Yale University Press.

Fischer, F. (1961). *Germany's aims in the first World War.* New York: Norton.

Fischer, F. (1975). *War of illusions* (M. Jackson, Trans.). New York: Norton.

Freedman, L., & Karsh, E. (1993). *The Gulf conflict, 1990/91.* Princeton, NJ: Princeton University Press.

George, A. L. (1989). A provisional theory of crisis management. In A. L. George (Ed.), *Avoiding war: Problems of crisis management* (pp. 22–27). Boulder, CO: Westview.

George A. L., & Smoke, R. (1974). *Deterrence in American foreign policy.* New York: Columbia University Press.

Herwig, H. H. (1987). Clio deceived: Patriotic self-censorship in Germany after the great war. *International Security, 12,* 5–44.

Huth, P. K. (1988). *Extended deterrence and the prevention of war.* New Haven, CT: Yale University Press.

Iriye, A. (1986). *The Origins of the second World War in Asia and the Pacific.* Essex, England: Longman.

Jervis, R. (1976). *Perception and misperception in international politics.* Princeton, NJ: Princeton University Press.

Jervis, R. (1988). War and misperception. *Journal of Interdisciplinary History, 18,* 675–700.

Kahneman, D., & Tversky, A. (1979). Prospect theory: an analysis of decision under risk. *Econometrica, 47,* 263–291.

Lebow, R. N. (1981). *Between peace and war.* Baltimore: Johns Hopkins University Press.

Levy, J. S. (1983). Misperception and the causes of war: Theoretical linkages and analytical problems. *World Politics, 36,* 75–99.

Levy, J. S. (1988). When do deterrent threats work? *British Journal of Political Science, 18,* 485–512.

Levy, J. S. (1989). The diversionary theory of war: A critique. In M. I. Midlarsky (Ed.), *Handbook of War Studies* (pp. 258–288). London: Allen & Unwin.

Levy, J. S. (1996). Loss aversion, framing, and bargaining: The implications of prospect theory for international conflict. *International Political Science Review, 17,* 177–193.

Levy, J. S. (1997). Prospect theory, rational choice, and international relations. *International Studies Quarterly, 41,* 87–112.

Levy, J. S. (1998). The causes of war and the conditions of peace. *Annual Review of Political Science, 1,* 139–166.

Maoz, Z. (1983). Resolve, capabilities, and the outcomes of international disputes, 1816–1976. *Journal of Conflict Resolution, 27,* 195–229.

Social Science Citation Index, 1996 Annual. (1997). Philadelphia: Institute for Scientific Information.

Vasquez, J. A. (1993). *The war puzzle.* New York: Cambridge University Press.

von Clausewitz, C. (1976). *On war* (M. Howard & P. Paret, Ed. and Trans.) Princeton, NJ: Princeton University Press.

Wang, K., & Ray, J. L. (1994). Beginners and winners: The fate of initiators of interstate wars involving great powers since 1495. *International Studies Quarterly, 38,* 139–154.

White, R. K. (1968). *Nobody wanted war: Misperception in Vietnam and other wars.* Garden City, NY: Doubleday/Anchor.

White, R. K. (1984). *Fearful warriors: A psychological profile of U.S.–Soviet relations.* New York: Free Press.

White, R. K. (Ed.). (1986). *Psychology and the prevention of nuclear war.* New York: New York University Prepreemptss.

PEACE AND CONFLICT: JOURNAL OF PEACE PSYCHOLOGY, 4(2), 137–141

Toward A Greater Focus on War's Alternatives

George Levinger

Department of Psychology
University of Massachusetts, Amherst

This commentary acknowledges Ralph White's valuable contributions to the psychological understanding of international conflict. It then addresses some of the problems of trying to evaluate the "results" of particular "acts of force," given the extremely complex contexts of each such act. It concludes with a discussion of non-coercive bases of power, whose strengthening would decrease the need to employ military force among nation states.

Ralph White has a distinguished record of analyzing issues of war and peace, especially the different parties' perceptions and misperceptions in international conflicts. He is one of only a handful of social psychologists who have made important contributions to the analysis of the psychological mechanisms that perpetuate military solutions to such conflicts. His current article builds on those previous insights in order to evaluate the consequences of 12 prominent American "acts of force" during the past 80 years. On the basis of several criteria, he rates each case's outcome on a continuum from good to bad, and he later discusses various sorts of misperceptions that lead to war. Thus, he continues to stimulate our consideration of important issues of war and peace.

I find much to agree with in White's analysis. If I were compelled to rate the outcomes of the same sample of the 12 "acts of force" considered in the main part of his article, my ratings would correlate highly with his. For example, both the United States' 1941 entrance into World War II and our 1995 armed intervention in Bosnia clearly appear more justifiable and more effective than our 1964–1974 actions in Vietnam or our support of the 1961 Bay of Pigs invasion. I also agree largely with White's list of conspicuous American international "sins"—from our leaders' ruinous demands on a defeated Germany at the time of the Versailles Treaty

Requests for reprints should be sent to George Levinger, University of Massachusetts, Department of Psychology, Box 37710, Amherst, MA 01003–7710.

in 1919 to their actions before and after the Persian Gulf War of 1991. Especially when viewed with hindsight, the listed cases are all instances where U.S. policy-makers made grave mistakes. Unfortunately, one can add many other instances to White's list of iniquities: for example, our invasions of Grenada and Panama during the 1980s; our covert support of Latin American death squads; and our military aid to corrupt regimes all around the globe, including the support of the current vicious oppression of native people in Mexico's Chiapas province. As White suggests, every such instance undercuts the United States' claims that our primary policy is to promote democracy in the world.

CRITIQUE

Nevertheless, I am troubled by several aspects of White's attempt to rate the results of American military actions. First, I wonder whether White's prescriptions might be read by policymakers as an endorsement of war as a justifiable instrument of foreign policy "as long as it works." Despite his own peaceful intentions to the contrary, could not some strategists consider White to be an incipient psychological Clausewitz, that is, someone who approves of war as long as it is conducted according to his principles?

Might such readers conclude that White would approve of the threat or use of military force whenever it is widely believed that (a) it has a "defensive" purpose, (b) it has a high degree of "world support," and (c) it seems close to 100% likely that it will achieve military victory? Conditions 1 and 3 have been claimed by war makers throughout history, even by Adolf Hitler. The remaining condition of receiving "world support" is more difficult to achieve, but smart leaders might be able to manipulate national and international opinion in their country's favor—especially when the war is poorly publicized or hidden away in central Africa or on a Pacific island.

Second, is the essentially post-hoc nature of such evaluations. For instance, White's Table 1 implies that military success is a necessary condition for rating an action as having had a "good" result. All of White's six cases with "good" outcomes were also militarily successful, whereas three fourths of his "bad"-result cases were militarily unsuccessful. In 9 out of 10 of these cases, then, White's ratings would parallel evaluations by conventional military leaders. The only exception is the mysterious 1973 SAC Alert, whose rating depends largely on its critique by secondary sources. One might ask, therefore: Can anyone devise independent theoretical criteria for evaluating the wisdom or folly of particular acts of force?

Third, there are inherent ambiguities in attempting to evaluate specific threats or uses of force. Each such instance has its roots in previous acts of force and each, no matter how immediately justifiable or successful, is likely to provoke new instances. It seems superfluous to remind ourselves that today's violence in Serbia, the Middle East, and elsewhere is rooted in much earlier violence or that its current handling will determine the likelihood of future violence. Any particular analysis is likely to be incomplete and, thus, controversial.

To illustrate that, I will briefly and incompletely discuss two of White's 12 cases. One pertains to America's joining the Allies in 1917 to fight Germany in World War I, whose outcome was rated as ambiguous. A second is our 1950 intervention after the North Korean army was driving the South Koreans into the sea, which was said to have a good result.

I believe that the U.S. intervention in 1917 was clearly instrumental in preventing Kaiser Wilhelm's Germany from defeating France and Britain in World War I; from that standpoint, it was highly successful. What was unsuccessful, however, was the war's aftermath. President Wilson's rigid demands, at Versailles, to extract huge reparations from the defeated Germany may have been morally justifiable, but they were economically ruinous; they far exceeded the most optimistic estimates of what the German post-war economy could possibly pay (e.g., Johnson, 1952, pp. 262–268). Yet, the foolishness of those post-war demands, and their destructive effects on the 1920s German Republic, should not affect our evaluation of America's military intervention 2 years earlier.

The 1950 Korean intervention was a consequence of an unclear American and United Nations policy in the preceding year or two (e.g., Manchester, 1978, pp. 540–543). U.S. policymakers had earlier signaled that they had little interest in shoring up the Republic of South Korea, and this gave North Korean leaders the distinct impression that they would be free to take over the South. For example, "congressional Republicans had fought all appropriations for Seoul [and in January, 1950, had helped defeat a] measure that would have provided ... U. S. Army officers to supervise the equipping of South Korean troops" (Manchester, 1978, p. 541). Furthermore, in early 1950, Secretary of State Acheson publicly announced America's Pacific defense perimeter as running from Japan's Ryuku Islands down to the Philippines, thereby ignoring South Korea.

Only after the subsequent invasion, in June 1950, did President Truman and others realize the full importance of maintaining the status quo. From that standpoint—and in terms of defense, world support, and later military success—General MacArthur's reconquest of South Korea's territory can be considered a "good" result of our act of force (Korean War—1st Phase). However, the need for this "act" could have been prevented by a more intelligent policy in earlier years. In other words, there had been no previous clear, internationally agreed on or enforceable policy concerning the consequences of international aggression in this geographic area. This vacuum helped create the misunderstanding that led the North Koreans—probably acting with Soviet encouragement—to invade the South in order to unify all of Korea under their rule.

ALTERNATIVES TO WAR:
A SOCIAL POWER PERSPECTIVE

Under the crisis circumstances faced by policymakers before and during the sorts of incidents sampled by White, there often are no choices except either passive appeasement or the active use of military force. Given those limitations, one may accept the use of force as a lesser evil. In this journal, however, we need not be so accepting. It is important for us to examine alternatives to military force. I turn, therefore, to a social psychological conception of force and power.

The threat or use of armed force is essentially the use of *coercive power*, or the ability of one party to punish the other for non-compliance (French & Raven, 1959). Most discussions of international policy—especially by political scientists—equate the use of force with coercion, and it is certainly the most dramatic and most widely applicable force. However, violence usually breeds further violence, and thus—no matter how immediately satisfying its results—coercive power alone is ultimately an undesirable basis of lasting influence.

Thus social psychologists have long recognized the importance of various other bases of power (e.g., French & Raven, 1959). People—including national leaders—do things not only because they want to avoid punishment but also because they wish to be rewarded (i.e., the other party's reward power), because they like or identify with the other party (referent power), because they think a request is right or legitimate (legitimate power), or both.[1]

In those terms, "acts of force" need not rely solely on coercion or the threat of coercion. Rather, they can be based on one or more other forms of social power. Party B is often influenced to do things for Party A for reasons that have little or nothing to do with actual or potential coercion.

Thus, successful acts of force often utilize an influencing party's (or nation's or coalition's) ability to reward the other—for example, A's granting a loan or supplying B with an important material need. Influence may be based on shared values or liking—for example, B's voting with A or speaking on behalf of A because the two parties share common interests. It may also be based on the legitimacy of the request—for example, when Parties A and B have a prior understanding, contract, or treaty that regulates their behavior toward each other. In international relations, the prevalence of legitimate acts of force is generally underestimated because they are undramatic and unremarkable; however, note the importance of postal or telecommunication agreements, or of air travel and maritime regulations, for the smooth functioning of international relations.

---

[1]Less germane to this discussion are "expert power," or the ability to influence another through one's own knowledge or expertise, and "information power," or the ability to influence by providing independent facts or information (see Raven, 1965).

War, especially total war, is the embodiment of pure mutual coercion, with a disappearance of alternate forms of influencing one's opponent. To prevent war requires nations to build, maintain, and use those other bases of mutual influence. It means strengthening the rewardingness of internation interdependence through trade and other mutually beneficial exchanges, furthering goodwill and shared interests to build referent power, and developing a mutually agreed on set of laws and principles for international conduct. On that basis, it is possible for armed forces to exist in the service of a higher law that embodies agreed on procedures for resolving disputes peacefully—the essential difference between policing and mere fighting.

The existence of a strong peaceful interdependence—which generally exists among friendly neighbors or trading partners—implies a reservoir of alternate bases of international power. Thus, the outcomes of World War II were, overall, more successful than those of World War I not because of the Western Allies' smashing victories over Germany and Japan but because of the establishment of high degrees of political and economic interdependence with the defeated nations, which helped overcome German or Japanese motives of further revenge or violence.

Nonetheless, the desire for national sovereignty and the economic greed of individuals, families, nations, and multinational corporations tend to undercut such constructive interdependence. They erode the advances toward international stability envisaged in the founding of international institutions such as the United Nations. They perpetuate the inequalities and resentments that destabilize peace. They encourage the buildup and maintenance of national military forces that consume a huge portion of the world's wealth and often serve to further diminish adherence to international law. It is to those issues that we need to turn our further attention.

REFERENCES

French, J. R. P., Jr., & Raven, B. (1959). The bases of social power. In D. Cartwright (Ed.), *Studies in social power*. Ann Arbor, MI: Institute for Social Research.

Johnson, A. (1952). *Pioneer's progress*. New York: Viking.

Manchester, W. (1978). *American Caesar: Douglas MacArthur, 1880–1964*. Boston: Little, Brown.

Raven, B. H. (1965). Social influence and power. In I. D. Steiner & M. Fishbein (Eds.), *Current studies in social psychology*. New York: Holt.

On the top of the priorities for action is a transformation which is perhaps the most difficult and far-reaching in history—the shift from a culture of war and violence to a culture of peace. It is a change which in earlier times would have been dismissed as utopian. But today, it can be seen as both feasible and indispensable for the future development—and even survival—of humanity.

Frederico Mayor,
Director-General,
UNESCO, 1995

PEACE AND CONFLICT: JOURNAL OF PEACE PSYCHOLOGY, 4(2), 143–147
Copyright © 1998, Lawrence Erlbaum Associates, Inc.

Some Questions and Comments About the Use of Force

Ethel Tobach

American Museum of Natural History, New York

The article "American Acts of Force: Results and Misperceptions" proposes a model for evaluating the relative effect of military force and threats of force in maintaining peace. It also raises some fundamental questions about U.S. actions and the relationship between individuals and society in formulating and carrying out international policies. This commentary offers some data about U.S. international activities and postulates the interdependence of individuals and nations in the making of history.

Being asked to write a commentary on a thought-provoking article by Ralph K. White, a leader in peace psychology, makes me regret that an oral give-and-take is not possible. I find myself asking questions while reading the article and regretting that I cannot hear the answers.

The article represents a partial result of a lifetime of activity, writing, and thinking about the elimination of war and the maintenance of peace. It proposes a framework for the analysis of U.S. government policy in international affairs and presents the results of that analysis in terms of success in maintaining or gaining peace. Here is a wealth of ideas and formulations. I have to choose among these, and, therefore, I comment on only two matters: criteria for evaluating and judging U.S. actions and the relationship between individual and national actions. I hope my comments will open a dialog on these issues.

The article is an exemplar of political psychology and in particular of peace psychology. It sets forth 12 incidents of U.S. acts of force, or threats of force, and their results and the misperceptions preceding and following those acts, with particular relevance for obtaining and maintaining peace. Can we limit actions that obtain or maintain peace or war only to military, armed conflict?

Requests for reprints should be sent to Ethel Tobach, American Museum of Natural History, Central Park West at 79th Street, New York, NY 10024–5192. E-mail: tobach@amnh.org

The scope and meaning of "peace psychology" is discussed often in the sessions of Division 48 at American Psycological Association meetings and elsewhere. Most of the time, I prefer the concept of a psychology that is concerned primarily with human societal activities to gain and maintain global peace by bringing about the prevention of, or the cessation of, economic, societal, diplomatic, or military policies that result in harming and destroying people. Acting towards the prevention or cessation of destructive policies is most salient today. Is it possible to analyze past events without considering whether policies other than use of military actions were actually effective in the maintenance or destruction of peace? Should actions carrying out such policies be part of the criteria for judging results of the United States's actual use or threat of use of force? For example, how would we judge the following events within the framework proposed by the author? The following list of some military, economic, diplomatic adventures, and clandestine military force and threats of force by the United States is a somewhat edited part of a listing by Spanier & Hook (1998):

1954:   Central Intelligence Agency overthrows Guatemala's left-wing government.
1958:   United States lands marines in Lebanon after Iraqi revolution.
1965:   United States intervenes in the Dominican Republic.
1970:   United States invades Cambodia.
1973:   Allende overthrown (role of the United States?).
1975:   United States places arms embargo on Turkey; embargo lifted in 1978.
1982:   United States intervenes in El Salvador and Nicaragua.
1983:   United States invades Grenada.
1984:   United States cuts off assistance to contras in Nicaragua; gives it back in 1986.
1986:   United States attacks Libya.
1987:   United States protects Kuwaiti oil tankers from Iran.
1988:   U.S. Navy shoots down Iranian commercial jetliner.
1989:   United States invades Panama.
1990:   Iraqi troops invade Kuwait, provoking condemnation and economic sanctions by the United Nations.
1991:   Iraq, refusing to withdraw from Kuwait, is forced out in 43 days by the U.S.-led UN coalition.
1992:   United States in Haiti.
1994:   Semipermissive occupation in Haiti.
1994:   United States forces deployed to Persian Gulf to deter invasion by Iraq of Kuwait.

(I am omitting any questions about the Middle East, Kurds, Rwanda-Hutu–Tutsi situation, the former Yugoslavia, and other contemporary problem areas.)

This listing makes me question Dr. White's statement that American military success and consequent power have served basic human values more than they have not. The interdependence of economic and cold war issues is apparent in this list of actions. Is it possible that these events were the outcome of policies dictated by such issues rather than high-minded beneficent values? I am reminded of a statement by Randolph Bourne cited by Howard Zinn (1980): "War is the health of the state" (p. 350).

Can one overlook the significance of economic issues in the formulation of the policies and actions? For example, the interrelation of military and economic policies is seen in a recent article in The New York Times. The headline reads: "As Asia's Economic Turmoil Deepens, Pentagon Chief Reassures Indonesia." The article reads

> Secretary of Defense William S. Cohen met here today with President Suharto to discuss expanding security ties with the beleaguered Indonesian Government. ... Mr. Suharto, who took power in a coup 32 years ago that left a reported 500,000 people died (sic!) has recently faced rare calls from opponents to step down....Officials here and those traveling with Mr. Cohen ... have repeatedly expressed concern that any further erosion of Indonesia's economy could lead to wide-spread unrest and even, in the worst case, the disintegration of a country. (Myers, 1998, p. D8)

It should be noted that Indonesia is a country with an execrable record of violation of the civil rights of the people of East Timor and various dissidents (Amnesty International). The record of exploitation of workers in the Asian sphere as a result of U.S. investments is well known. What is the stability that is being sought? Calls by civil rights groups for economic pressure on Indonesia to change their policies towards the people of East Timor have fallen on deaf ears in the U.S. government.

In light of such formidable processes as the globalization of the U.S. economy, how are we to understand the relation between the actions of individuals and nations in the international processes of peace and war? Dr. White is clearly concerned for the global welfare of humanity. Yet, he gives much emphasis to the psychology and personality of the individual leaders or their advisors, and the nations are described in psychological terms, thereby "psychologizing" national policies and international relations. Is there an implicit, fundamental assumption that the personality and psychology of individuals, that is, the leaders or their advisors, are the major factors in national policymaking?

The policies of the U.S. government dictated by the military–industrial elite for maintaining its power and dominance over the lives of the peoples of the world take many forms. It is these policies that underlie the choice of leaders that are put before the public for their vote. That the individuals chosen by the military–industrial elite are not always controllable and their behavior predictable is a function of the intersection of two lines of dialectical development: One is that produced by the processes by which the class in power is united or disunited by competing economic interests within itself; the other is that produced by the processes by which an individual comes to sufficient prominence to be seen as a possible candidate for governing the state. The social and societal processes that make a Clinton or a Reagan the choice of the power elite are interwoven with the class processes that produce a two-party system. When these two lines of development cross, individual and national actions take place, and history is made. In other words, when the organization and expression of class interests are integrated with the personal behavior and characteristics of the appointed leader, international policies are implemented. However, it is probable that the final decisions are consonant with the goals of the class that produced the leader and the advisors.

A recent Hollywood film, Wag the Dog, is a satirical explication of the ways in which these lines of development are orchestrated to produce "international events." In this film, a "fake" war is presented to the public as a distraction from an imminent scandal in the White House. Unfortunately, in real life, the war may not be "fake" and may be a distraction from other matters that concern public welfare.

What can psychologists study to understand the politics and psychology of peace and war (see deRivera, 1968, for an attempt to integrate political science, history, and psychology)? Should they study small group psychology (Semmel, 1982)? Individual psychology (Klineberg, 1964; Lyons, 1997; Schafer, 1997)? Should they study the individual physiologically and society biologically (Hopple, 1980; 1982; Tobach, 1988; 1990; 1991; Wiegele, 1982)? How can they integrate the social and societal development of the individuals of the various classes who as leaders become players in the formation of public policy (e.g., the role of the leaders of the peace movement in the ending of the Vietnam war)? (See Kelman, 1979, for a statement of the need to identify the level of analysis, i.e., the role of the individual in relation to the nation.) Is one of the important factors in the gaining and maintenance of peace the development of parties and movements that prevent the development of policies that are destructive? Could that be a factor in the "success" of a state's international policy?

Can peace psychologists play a role in achieving that "success?" Should peace psychologists play a role in that process? I think so.

REFERENCES

de Rivera, J. (1968). *The psychological dimension of foreign policy.* Columbus, Ohio: Merrill.

Hopple, G. W. (1980). *Political psychology and biopolitics: Assessing and predicting elite behavior in foreign policy.* Boulder, CO: Westview.

Hopple, G. W. (1982). *Biopolitics, political psychology, and international politics.* New York: St. Martin's.

Kelman, H. (1979). The Forum, selected and edited excerpts from the Plenary Session on Ethical and Social Responsibility in the Practice of Political Psychology [Comments]. *Political Psychology, 1,* 100–102.

Klineberg, O. (1964). *The human dimension in international politics.* New York: Holt, Rinehart, & Winston.

Lyons, M. (1997). Presidential character revisited. *Political Psychology, 18,* 791.

Myers, S. L. (1998, January 15). As Asia's economic turmoil deepens, pentagon chief reassures Indonesia. *New York Times,* p. D8.

Schafer, M. (1997). Images and policy preferences. *Political Psychology, 18,* 813–829.

Semmel, A. K. (1982). Small group dynamics in foreign policymaking. In G. W. Hopple (Ed.), *Biopolitics, political psychology, and international politics* (pp. 94–113). New York: St. Martin's Press.

Spanier, J. W., & Hook, S. W. (1998). *American foreign policy since World War II* (14th ed.). Washington, DC: CQ Press.

Tobach, E. (1988). Biology and social sciences. *Nature, Society and Thought, 1,* 587–596.

Tobach, E. (1990). Biologie und Sozialwissenschaften [Biology and social science]. In H. J. Sandkuhler (Ed.), *Europaeische Enzyklopadie zu Philosophie und Wissenschaften.* Hamburg, Germany: Verlag.

Tobach, E. (1991). The politics of biopolitics: a review essay. *Nature, Society, and Thought, 4,* 491–505.

Tobach, E. (1994). Personal is political. *Journal of Social Issues, 50,* 221–244.

Tobach, E. (1995). The science of peace and the peace of science. Presentation to Division 48, American Psychological Association meeting.

Wiegele, T. C. (1982). The case for a biological perspective in the study of international relations. In G. W. Hopple (Ed.), *Biopolitics, political psychology, and international politics* (pp. 151–173). New York: St. Martin's.

Zinn, H. (1980). *A people's history of the United States.* New York: Harper.

Whatever the reason why psychologists and others have neglected the topic of children and political violence in the past, today the need for a higher research profile for this area is greater than ever.

Ed Cairns, 1996

PEACE AND CONFLICT: JOURNAL OF PEACE PSYCHOLOGY, 4(2), 149–154
Copyright © 1998, Lawrence Erlbaum Associates, Inc.

Vintage White: Comments on "American Acts of Force: Results and Misperceptions"

Richard V. Wagner
Department of Psychology
Bates College

White's article on American acts of force is consistent with much of his writing over the past years, especially the themes he chooses, the methodology of his analyses, and his approach to his audience. I commend much of White's latest effort, indicate concern about the criteria White uses to determine the success of acts of force, and conclude with a discussion of the relevance of White's analysis to the study of peace and conflict in the 21st century.

There is a remarkable consistency to almost every article or book Ralph White has produced over his 60 distinguished years of scholarship—from the landmark studies of leadership style (Lewin, Lippitt, & White, 1939) through the analyses of World War II propaganda (e.g., White, 1949), cognitive and motivational factors involved in Vietnam (White, 1966), and the Cold War (White, 1984) to the conflicts of the 1990s in the Persian Gulf (White, 1991a) and in Bosnia (White, 1996). His article, "American Acts of Force: Results and Misperceptions" is no exception. It is, in most respects, vintage White: timely, relevant, and challenging. It is with great delight and respect that I offer this commentary on Ralph White's latest contribution to social, political, and peace psychology.

My commentary will be in three parts. First, I will reflect on how this article is consistent with White's past efforts, especially with respect to the themes, the methodology, and the audience for whom he writes. Second, I will comment on the concerns I have about his analysis. Then, I will conclude by discussing the relevance of this article to the emerging field of peace psychology as it moves into the 21st

Requests for reprints should be sent to Richard V. Wagner, Department of Psychology, Bates College, Lewiston, ME 04240. E-mail: rwagner@bates.edu.

century, especially with respect to the increasing importance of non-national ethnic conflict and the recognition of systemic conflict at the end of the Cold War era.

THEMES

Ralph White's analysis of "American acts of force" is in keeping with the themes he has treated over the years. For the most part, the themes have been characterized by timeliness and political relevance. Although the original Lewin, Lippitt, and White (1939) studies of autocratic, democratic, and laissez-faire leadership styles pertained to the emerging field of group dynamics and were based in Lewinian field theory, their relevance to political leadership in the late 1930s is unmistakable. In his (White, 1949) analysis of war propaganda as used by Hitler and Franklin Roosevelt, White concludes with speculation about how his analysis can be applied to Soviet propaganda. His examination (White, 1966) of misperception and the Vietnam War was certainly timely, as was his analysis of Soviet–U.S. relations, *Fearful Warriors* (White, 1984). Timeliness and political relevance are nowhere more apparent than in his before–after analyses of the conduct of the Persian Gulf War (White, 1991a, 1991b).

This article, White's review of American acts of force, is obviously politically relevant, although it might appear more historical than the typical White product, covering as it does "12 American acts of force" from World War I to the Bosnian conflict. Nevertheless, White maintains his record of timeliness by applying his principles to a contemporary case of ethnic conflict (Bosnia) and offering guidelines for future policy.

METHODOLOGY

White's methodology is not traditional psychological methodology. His methodological style can be loosely termed qualitative with a hint of what one might call "personal quantitativeness." Reviewing, as I did, several of White's early qualitative analyses culled from ancient, yellowing copies of the *Journal of Abnormal and Social Psychology* stored in the attic of the Bates College library, I found that he used to employ "value-analysis," a scoring procedure for quantifying references to goals and values contained in written documents. In one case, it was an analysis of Richard Wright's *Black Boy* (White, 1947) and, in the other, the aforementioned analysis of Hitler's and Roosevelt's war propaganda (White, 1949).

Frankly, I do not know when White abandoned value-analysis, but it seems to me that he internalized the methodology and has implicitly applied it in his analyses of misperceptions in Vietnam, the Cold War, the Persian Gulf, Bosnia, and now, retrospectively, other major "American acts of force" in the 20th century. His data have gone from specific objects of analysis (e.g., the pages of *Black Boy*, specific U.S. and Nazi propaganda statements) to the facts surrounding international political events as represented in the wide variety of "expert sources" he has read in preparing his analysis. His methodology is subjective. He decides who is an expert and selects the sources; he interprets what they report; he keeps an internal account I am sure of the agreement among his sources; and then he reports, often without specific citation, the "results" of this subjective qualitative procedure. Although such a subjective procedure could lead to nothing more than glorified editorial statements on political issues, in White's case I do not think it does. In fact, I see great value in his type of analysis for several reasons. First, and very importantly, by bringing to bear a sort of metanalysis of others' reports and expert interpretations, he shows how psychologists can extend the scope of their analyses to themes they seldom study, to wit, very real political events and the people involved in them. If knowledgeable experts agree, for example, that the Bay of Pigs was a disaster and that the Kennedy administration ignored Central Intelligence Agency warnings about the likelihood that the Cuban people would rally around an invading exile force, then we can begin to apply psychological principles to the misperception and miscalculation in the U.S. response to the Cuban dilemma. We do not have to have been in the briefing or war rooms sounding out each policymaker's views of the decision process. Second, the reports and analyses he uses come from experts in a variety of fields, especially diplomacy, history, political science, sociology, and economics. The more interdisciplinary the analyses, the better for psychology. Third, White grounds much of his interpretation of the experts' reports in psychological theory, specifically applying cognitive and motivational concepts to his data. Finally, he reports his sources—the books (usually) and journals from which he has culled his data. In the right hands (and White's hands are right!), such a methodology can provide a very stimulating analysis of very real, meaningful events.

AUDIENCE

A third characteristic of Ralph White's scholarship is that he tries to challenge his audiences. In his analysis of Hitler and Roosevelt war propaganda, he shows many of the similarities between the two leaders' styles, something I suspect few social scientists were inclined to consider so soon after the war. In his analysis of misperception in Vietnam, published in 1966 before U.S. actions in southeast Asia were under national assault, he argues that both the U.S. and the Vietnamese misperceived one another, that our U.S. assumptions about North Vietnamese aggression might be questioned. In 1984, *Fearful Warriors* challenged political scientists to think psychologically and psychologists to turn their attention to the political arena. In 1986, he published an article in the *International Journal of Intelligence and Counterintelligence*, urging the intelligence community to recognize the importance of realistic empathy in assessing one's adversaries. In this article, he challenges peace psychologists to take a second look at the effectiveness of war—in some cases. Being controversial has never been a problem for Ralph White, to our benefit.

CONCERNS ABOUT "AMERICAN ACTS OF FORCE"

I have two concerns about White's analysis of "American acts of force." First, there are problems with several of the criteria White uses to determine "good results" of force. One criterion is *military success*, "to the extent that it leads to ... low cost in terms of death, physical suffering, and economic deprivation." The lower the loss of life and physical suffering the better, of course, but the question for me is "relative to what?" It may be, for example, that U.S. entry into World War I hastened the capitulation of the Austrian and German armies, with relatively low cost of U.S. lives. However, we do not know whether increased diplomatic initiatives might have accomplished a cessation of hostilities with almost no loss of U.S. lives. It is an analysis that cannot be made. Because no comparison is possible, there is no way to counter the claim that U.S. entry into a war was a military success because of the low loss of life. Such an analysis, as I'm sure White recognizes, is not scientific.

A second criterion White applies is *peace*, defined "as ending a war, hastening the end of a war, deterring an attack that would otherwise precipitate a war." When do you consider a war to have ended? When the hostilities present at the time of the act of force cease? White apparently thinks so, given his use of the example of U.S. intervention in Bosnia. A strong argument can be made that the United States has merely suppressed the hostilities for the time being and, as soon as U.S. forces leave, hostilities will resume. Of course, those forces could remain for decades, as peacekeepers have in Cyprus and the Gaza strip. Not only is the definition of peace arguable, but so is its meaning. As Salem (1993) has pointed out, Western policies directed toward peace may be seen elsewhere "as merely stratagems for defusing opposition to and rejection of the status quo" (p. 362).

Two other criteria of "good results" are democracy ("human rights, especially freedom of expression and majority rule") and national independence ("absence of subjugation of one nation by another"). The problem with these criteria is that they are culturally based. *Democracy* can take many forms, as we know. The Western form includes human rights, freedom of expression, and majority rule, but are these characteristics equally appropriate everywhere? Are they absolutes? They are for me, but need they be so for everyone? Human rights and freedom of expression are easier to promote in prosperous Western nations than in less developed nations elsewhere. The Western model is often applied without regard for or acknowledgement of its cultural base.

My concern about *national independence* is rooted in the definitions of both nation and independence. In the Second World War, the Allies "liberated" many areas of the Middle East, but did they liberate nations? Or ethnic groups? Or family dynasties? They drew lines in the sand, apparently somewhat arbitrarily, and declared the resultant territories nations. In the process, of course, they forced various alienated groups together under the same national umbrella, setting the stage for much of the turmoil the Middle East has experienced ever since. In other cases, they liberated areas that were then redominated by "alien rule": defeating the Japanese in Vietnam allowed the French to reassert their control, even if temporarily.

My second concern about White's analysis is more general and arises from his own question: "Are the advocates of non-violence right when they believe that almost any use or threat of international force is likely to do more harm than good?" Should we be questioning the value of the use of force under any but the most extreme circumstances? I am glad he raises the question, but, as I indicated earlier, I do not consider his analysis a fair test of the question, there being no true comparison possible. In many instances, force or the threat of force becomes an important alternative only because more positive, constructive ways of handling conflict were not implemented sufficiently early in the process. By focussing on the success of military force, thereby legitimizing it, White risks diverting us from the more important question of how we build mechanisms that promote positive intergroup relations that make acts of force unnecessary.

IMPLICATIONS FOR PEACE PSYCHOLOGY

The end of the Cold War has meant not only the end of the big power, Soviet–U.S. confrontation, it has signalled the end of international conflict as we have known it. At the moment, we are not at all sure what to discard from our old ways of thinking and not sure what to adopt as new. "We are," as Rasmussen (1997) states, "somewhere between paradigms" (p. 45). We can no longer analyze war and peace strictly in terms of nations, as the sad events in Bosnia and Rwanda, to pick just two examples, have clearly taught us. Intranational struggles direct us to question whether national boundaries are meaningful. Multiple groups have stakes in conflict throughout the world: nation–states, ethnic and religious groups, and a host of international interest groups such as economic blocs and ecological non-governmental organizations. The players are myriad, the relations among them more and more complex. Furthermore, peace and conflict can be conceptualized not only in terms of overt acts of violence but increasingly in terms of systemic, structural forms of violence, especially deriving from an economic system that rewards those who impress thousands of women and children in forced labor shops, for example, and promotes an increasing distance between the income of a very few people who are wealthy and the multitudes who are poverty stricken worldwide. Peace psychology must become a part of the reconceptualization necessary for psychological analyses of peace and conflict to be relevant in the next century.

How does Ralph White's analysis of "American acts of force" contribute to such a reconceptualization? First, he emphasizes, as always, the importance of misperception in conflict and urges us to go beyond the conventional view of the adversary, to perceive as veridically as possible the viewpoint of the other. The logical extension of this approach should lead us to recognize the cultural (as opposed to national) basis for the other's perception of the conflict, to see that there may be disagreements within the adversary camp, and to see that those disagreements might be based on different intranational perspectives. The nation–state may not be the critical unit of analysis, as the United States apparently recognized in establishing the coalition that attacked Iraq and urged Israeli forbearance in the Persian Gulf War. White's analysis here and in his thoughtful explanation (White, 1996) of "why the Serbs fought", shows his recognition of the importance of ethnic, non-national loyalties in one critical instance of protracted conflict. Second, in his discussion of how to determine a "good result" of a war, he specifically notes the increasing irrelevance of national boundaries: "Wars tend to spread; war refugees overflow national boundaries; diseases spread." Third, he includes "world support" as an important factor in evaluating the success of a war. This, too, moves us away from a strictly national perspective. Finally, although it is clear that White's analysis is made in the context of international conflict as conducted in the 1900s, in a sense, in this article, he has taken the ultimate 20th century step, calling us one last time to analyze the value of war as it has been traditionally conducted by the most powerful military nation now in existence. Where do we go from here? Off in search of new paradigms for 2001 and beyond.

REFERENCES

Lewin, K., Lippitt, R., & White, R. K. (1939). Patterns of aggressive behavior in experimentally created "social climates". *Journal of Social Psychology, 10,* 271–299.

Rasmussen, J. L. (1997). Peacemaking in the twenty-first century: New rules, new roles, new actors. In I. W. Zartman & J. L. Rasmussen (Eds.), *Peacemaking in international conflict: Methods and techniques* (pp. 23–50). Washington, DC: U.S. Institute of Peace Press.

Salem, P. E. (1993). A critique of Western conflict resolution from a non-Western perspective. *Negotiation Journal, 9,* 361–369.

White, R. K. (1947). Black Boy: A value-analysis. *Journal of Abnormal and Social Psychology, 42,* 440–461.

White, R. K. (1949). Hitler, Roosevelt, and the nature of war propaganda. *Journal of Abnormal and Social Psychology, 44,* 157–174.

White, R. K. (1966). Misperception and the Vietnam war [Entire issue]. *Journal of Social Issues, 22(3).*

White, R. K. (1984). *Fearful warriors: A psychological profile of U.S.–Soviet relations.* New York: Free Press.

White, R. K. (1986). Empathy as an intelligence tool. *International Journal of Intelligence and Counterintelligence, 1,* 57–75.

White, R. K. (1991a). Empathizing with Saddam Hussein. *Political Psychology, 12,* 291–308.

White, R. K. (1991b). End-of-war update. *Political Psychology, 12,* 465–466.

White, R. K. (1996). Why the Serbs fought: Motives and misperceptions. *Peace and Conflict: Journal of Peace Psychology, 2,* 109–128.

PEACE AND CONFLICT: JOURNAL OF PEACE PSYCHOLOGY, 4(2), 155–166

The Effects of Interpersonal Oppressive Violence on Women and Children: Implications for Conflict Management and Violence Prevention Training

Jennifer P. Maxwell

Center for Applied Conflict Management
Kent State University

This article presents a model for understanding interpersonal oppression and violence utilized specifically for the purpose of exercising coercive control over a victim—as is the case in domestic violence, rape, and child abuse. The deliberate use of violence for oppression is contrasted with the widely held view, in conflict management and violence prevention curricula, that people resort to violence because they lack alternative skills. The motivation of the perpetrator is explored and the effects of oppression on the victim is outlined, with particular attention to the disabling effects of trauma that render victims unable to effectively utilize conflict management skills developed in the context of a rational approach. The need for an increased awareness of oppressive violence on the part of conflict management and violence prevention practitioners is highlighted.

Conflict management, violence prevention, and aggression control programs share the common problem of addressing how to deal with interpersonal violence and aggression. Curricula materials are designed to teach people more effective ways to handle potentially violent situations or to control their own aggressive responses to conflict. Currently, the standard mode of dealing with these problems is by use of the rational approach. For reasons given later, however, this approach has serious shortcomings for coping with situations of interpersonal oppressive violence. This article examines some of the ways that the field of conflict management can benefit from a more complete understanding of this phenomenon so that more effective strategies can be devised for dealing with the problem of interpersonal oppressive violence.

Requests for reprints should be sent to Jennifer P. Maxwell, Center for Applied Conflict Management, Kent State University, 302 Bowman Hall, Kent, OH 44242. E-mail: jmaxwell@kent.edu

THE RATIONAL APPROACH

Conflict management and violence prevention programs typically approach the problems of interpersonal violence and aggression through teaching and training. Topics considered include the physiological response to anger and the "fight or flight" response to threat, as well as alternatives to fighting or fleeing—"talking it out," "making choices," "thinking before you act" (Copeland, 1989; Holmberg & Halligan, 1992; Ohio Youth Services Network, 1993; Prothrow-Stith, 1987; Sadalla, Henriquez & Holmberg, 1987). Each of these curricula emphasizes the importance of approaching situations in a rational manner.

This emphasis on rationality serves two important functions. The first is to enable the individual in a conflict situation to make a more informed choice of action and, hopefully, to choose the course of action that will both protect one's own interests as well as respect the interests of the other party. This concept of "enlightened self-interest" (Lax & Sebenius, 1986; Rubin, 1991; Susskind & Cruickshank, 1987) and related concepts—"principled negotiation" (Fisher & Ury, 1981) and "integration" (Follett, 1942)—enables both parties to meet their needs, as opposed to a situation that fosters a "winner" and a "loser." The second function of the emphasis on rationality is that by "thinking before you react," individuals can curb their impulse to fight or flee. In instances in which individuals tend to either react aggressively without considering the consequences of their actions or to "automatically" flee the situation (again, without regard for potential negative consequences), training in techniques to promote "thinking before you act" are intended to assist in impulse control through the exercise of rational thought and choice. A fundamental tenet of these programs is that violence can be curbed by teaching rational alternatives.

The emphasis placed on rationality by conflict management, violence prevention, and aggression control programs implies some interesting presuppositions about why violence is employed. If violence is used because it is either the easiest, or the most expedient, or the most familiar means to achieve the desired end, then teaching people alternative methods of meeting their needs and interests (achieving their ends) will be an effective alternative to violence. However, if the use of the "means" is the point, then an alternative to violence will not suffice; participation in violence is the point. In this situation, instruction in alternatives to violence will not work because participation in violence is the desired goal, rather than merely the means to the end. Violence is, therefore, both the *means* to exert control over another person, as well as the desired *end-state*. If this is the case, then teaching skills will not prevent violence because the lack of skills is not why violence is occurring.

The use of education regarding alternatives to violence is an appropriate model when violence is occurring from a lack of impulse control or lack of knowledge of alternatives. In these situations, individuals resorting to violence can be taught to control their impulses through behavior management techniques (i.e., attention to the physiological warning signs of anger, relaxation, aggression control) and the use of alternative strategies (i.e., listening and communication skills, assertiveness, negotiation, conflict management). However, education in alternatives to violence is both wholly inadequate, and can, in fact, revictimize the victim of violence (as will be discussed in the following sections), if it is used to address violence that is utilized by the perpetrator for the primary purpose of establishing control over the victim. For when violence is wielded for the purpose of subjugating the will of the victim to the will of the perpetrator, the relationship between the victim and the perpetrator is a relationship of oppression.

The violence of oppression is fundamentally different from violence used by a perpetrator to advance his own interests and goals, but in which the subjugation of the victim is not among those goals. The intent of the perpetrator is central to this distinction. This distinction hinges on the consideration of the following questions:

1. Is the perpetrator simply trying to maximize his interests in the most familiar manner (in this case, through the use of violence)? If the answer to this question is "Yes," then the perpetrator may very well be open to considering alternative strategies that would potentially allow a more egalitarian process of goal attainment to take place—the exercise of enlightened self-interest.

2. Is the perpetrator using violence to control and subjugate the victim—is the goal the subjugation of the victim? If the answer to this question is "Yes," then teaching the perpetrator more non-violent methods of goal attainment will only serve, at best, to give the perpetrator an expanded arsenal of techniques for controlling the victim. (As one of the author's university students said, referring to Ury's book *Getting Past No* (1991), "Yeah, these techniques are perfect for helping me 'get past no' when I'm trying to lay some broad and she's into 'no'; KSU student, personal communication, March 13, 1995) Written over a century ago, the historic statement by Nietzsche (1956) offers a portrayal of the perpetrator's "pleasure" in the subjugation of the will of another:

> That pleasure is induced by his being able to exercise his power freely upon one who is powerless, by the pleasure of *faire le mal pour le plaisir de le faire*, the pleasure of violation [or the pleasure of rape] (p. 196).

THE PERPETRATORS

Who are these perpetrators? Herman (1997) states that the perpetrator's "most consistent feature, in both the testimony of victims and the observations of psychologists, is his apparent normality" (p. 75). This characteristic of the perpetrator is perhaps the most horrifying—psychologically, nothing has been found to differentiate perpetrators from normal individuals:

Sensitive to the realities of power and to social norms, . . . [the perpetrator is rarely in] difficulties with the law; rather, he seeks out situations where his tyrannical behavior will be tolerated, condoned, or admired. His demeanor provides an excellent camouflage, for few people believe that extraordinary crimes can be committed by men of such conventional appearance. (Herman, 1997, p. 75)

If these "conventional" perpetrators were scarce, and if the violence inherent in the process of objectification and in the "pleasure of oppression"—of *faire le mal pour le plaisir de le faire*—was an uncommon occurrence, perhaps it would be of less consequence. However, for women, the statistics for sexual assault, rape, and domestic violence are horrifyingly high. Research by Diana Russell (1984) found that one in four women had been raped and one in three women had been sexually abused in childhood. The majority of women (78%) are victimized, not by strangers, but by persons known to them—husbands, exhusbands, boyfriends, exboyfriends (29%); relatives (9%); acquaintances (40%) (Bureau of Justice Statistics, 1995). The leading cause of injury for women ages 15–44 is domestic violence, more than car accidents, rapes, and muggings combined (Congressional Record, 1993). "Nearly one-fourth of American women will be abused by a current or former partner at some point in their lives" (Women's Action Coalition [WAC] Stats, 1993, p. 55). In cases where the victim–offender relationship is known, 26% of female murder victims were killed by their husbands or boyfriends (Federal Bureau of Investigation Crime Reports, 1995); the National Clearinghouse for the Defense of Battered Women places the number of women killed by their husbands or boy-friends at more than one third of female homicide victims (WAC Stats, 1993).

The statistics on violence against women, however high they appear, are considered to be gross underestimates by the very agencies that produce them. The FBI estimates that only about 10% of domestic violence is reported to the police (WAC Stats, 1993)—"In the United States the FBI believes that domestic violence is the most under reported crime and estimates that it is probably ten times more under reported than rape" (Hague & Malos, 1993, p. 11). Rape, however, is also grossly under reported; the National Victim Center and Crime Victims Research and Treatment Center report that "it is estimated that 85% of rapes are never reported to the police" (WAC Stats, 1993, p. 49). Violence against women is a pervasive and under-acknowledged reality in our society.

THE VIOLENCE OF OPPRESSION AND THE RATIONAL APPROACH

The violence of oppression is not amenable to change through the application of enlightened self-interest. The pursuit of oppression is antithetical to the pursuit of enlightened self-interest. Conflict management and violence prevention programs do victims a disservice by not addressing the motivation for violence that is at the heart of domestic violence, the form of violence predominately affecting women and children. This disservice is done in two ways:

1. The perpetrator is presumed to be a "victim" of his lack of appropriate skills. The assumption is made that violence, on the part of the perpetrator, can be addressed through the acquisition of skills and the exercise of rationality—"thinking before you act"—in order to minimize harm to the victim and ultimately allow for a more egalitarian relationship that maximizes gain for both parties. However, this is in direct contradiction to the actual motivation of the perpetrator, which is to subjugate and dominate the victim. The motivation to subjugate another human being is not a problem of having a deficient repertoire of skills. The theory that educating the perpetrator in more egalitarian modes of interaction will persuade him to choose to change his behavior neglects to take into account the fact that he chose his behavior precisely because it was oppressive and domineering. He was not forced into his behavior by a limited repertoire of skills but rather chose that behavior for its utility.

2. Neglecting to address the motivation behind domestic violence has a profound effect on the victim. It reinforces the erroneous assumption, on the part of the victim, that a quest for a rational resolution based on the concept of enlightened self-interest is possible and that there is a possibility, in this profoundly unequal relationship, for the needs of both parties to be met. As the following section illustrates, this belief merely compounds the damage to the victim, which is inherent in the perpetrator–victim relationship. Teaching an individual who is being exploited "win–win" negotiation, conflict management, and communication skills inadvertently magnifies the unrealistic belief of the victim that she is able, by her concerted efforts, to effect a change in the perpetrator–victim relationship. This unrealistic view is already a part of the pathology of trauma and is one of the mechanisms that keeps the victim entrenched as a victim.

The magnitude of the problem—teaching conflict management skills without including an exploration of the power relationship between perpetrator and victim—is increased by the growing use of conflict management and violence prevention curricula materials as a primary method in addressing the problem of violence. Often, the institution of a violence prevention or conflict management curriculum is the primary response of a school system, or a juvenile facility, to teach more prosocial and non-violent methods of dealing with violence. However, without a profound understanding of these very different motivations for violence, and without a full understanding that the pursuit of enlightened self-interest is highly inappropriate in some situations, these curricula have the potential to further disempower the very people they seek to instruct.

The problem is even more complex. When conflict management and violence prevention curricula do address the existence of a perpetrator, the emphasis is on a recognizable perpetrator—the bully that is clearly a bully and can be dealt with as a bully in a variety of ways. Resist the bully through assertively refusing to comply ("saying 'No'"), change the dynamics of the interaction so that the bully is encouraged to change his behavior, and educate the bully in conflict management skills and enlightened self-interest (Copeland, 1989; Holmberg & Halligan, 1992; Ohio Youth Services Network, 1993; Prothrow-Stith, 1987; Sadalla, Henriquez, & Holmberg, 1987). Even if these tactics did not contain the flaws discussed in the previous section, the utilization of these skills is triggered by the recognition of the bully as a bully. However, when the perpetrator approaches the victim in the guise of a "relationship"—whether "friend," "lover," "parent," or "husband"—the victim is not prompted to make use of any skills of resistance or to seek help because there is no perception of danger.

DISSOCIATED COERCION AND TRAUMA

As previously stated, threats of violence to young women in the form of domestic violence and sexual assault are significantly more likely to come from persons known to them than from strangers. Even though assault and violence prevention programs address the fact that in four out of five cases the perpetrators of violence are known to the victim (Bureau of Justice Statistics, 1995; National Assault Prevention Center, 1986), most of the self-defense and conflict resolution techniques are designed to be used against perpetrators who are recognizable as opponents. There is an assumption made that the victim will recognize the perpetrator as someone who intends to cause harm and can then employ the appropriate self-defense strategies (i.e., a rational assessment of whether or not I am at risk and, if so, what strategy I should adopt, etc.). Without the ability to first assess the situation and then to decide on an appropriate response, these techniques are useless. Research on rape, battering and child sexual assault indicates that to assume that the victim recognizes the perpetrator as a perpetrator is an erroneous assumption in many cases, precisely because the offender is known to the victim and is considered an acquaintance, friend, or intimate. The ability of the victim to discern and to grasp the situation is lost; the perpetrator is not recognizable as a perpetrator.

The overwhelming control of the victim by the perpetrator is often established by the juxtaposition of trust and violation or, in other words, by the use of "dissociated coercion" (Maxwell, 1996). In situations of battering and sexual abuse, the perpetrator approaches the victim from a trust-based perspective, professing to offer love, comfort, or reassurance while simultaneously violating the victim by breaking that trust with assault, violence, and rape. The intent of the perpetrator is veiled and is often not apparent to the victim who, in struggling to make sense out of a situation that includes both trust and the violation of trust, increasingly manifests symptoms of psychological dissociation and trauma (Herman, 1997; van der Kolk, 1989). Without a "recognizable perpetrator," the inability to act from lack of recognition is coupled with the effect of trauma to disable the victim's normal "fight or flight" response; the victim is put in a position to be chronically and repeatedly victimized—as is typically the case with victims of battering and sexual abuse.

THE SHATTERING OF THE "FIGHT OR FLIGHT" SYSTEM OF SELF-PROTECTION

Exposure to dissociated coercion—the juxtaposition of trust and violation—disables the victim's ability to make use of the information offered in violence prevention and conflict management curricula. These curricula start with the assumption of the "fight or flight" response and seek to enlarge it with the addition of rational choice—"I can choose to fight, or choose to flee, or choose to negotiate, or choose to do whatever is best in this situation; I can choose my response." However, traumatic events such as rape, battering, and sexual assault overwhelm and shatter the normal physiological "fight or flight" response to danger. In situations in which the victim trusts the perpetrator, the tendency for the violent act to psychologically harm the victim is increased, precisely because it increases the overwhelming sense for the victim of "How could this be happening to me; how could this person, who I trust, be doing this to me?" Quite literally, the victim cannot assimilate what is happening (Horowitz, 1986) with her view of the perpetrator as her "friend;" the violent event simply does not "fit." For the victim to make sense of an event that inherently makes no sense and for her to understand the coupling of two mutually exclusive states—trust and violation—the victim fragments or "dissociates" the memory of the overwhelming event.

Dissociation is central to the traumatic reaction, or post-traumatic stress disorder (van der Kolk, MacFarlane, & Weisaeth, 1996). The traumatic event, by definition, is an event in which the victim has no choice; she is unable to escape—often because the victim has not perceived that she was in danger within the context of the interpersonal relationship until it is too late. The normal system of self-protection, designed to enable the victim to escape, is torn apart and replaced by disconnected physiological sensations, thoughts, emotions, and memories (Herman, 1997; van der Kolk, MacFarlane, & Weisaeth, 1996). For example, the resulting effect of the fragmentation of the "fight and flight" response for a rape victim can be that she does not consciously remember that she was raped (Spiegel, 1989). This is particularly apt to be the case when the perpetrator is a trusted "friend." Again, the juxtaposition of trust and violation is inconceivable to the victim—"how could someone who you trust want to violate and hurt you?" The thought just does not "make sense;" the victim literally "does not see it" due to the dissociating effects of trauma. It is not just that the victim does not want to recognize that her "friend" is a perpetrator of violation; the effect of the shattering of her system of self-protection is that she cannot see it—her reaction of terror and fear are not consciously connected to anything that she can remember the perpetrator doing (Harvey & Herman, 1994; Herman, 1995; Herman & Schatzow, 1987; Williams, 1994, 1995).

Therefore, the victim is doubly disabled with respect to her ability to recognize and name the situation for what it is. First, in the mind of the victim, there is a cognitive dissonance inherent in the combination of trust and violation. Second, the physiological "fight or flight" response is rendered useless by the perpetrator. This system of self-protection, prevented from the normal function of protecting the victim from actual harm, fragments into an abnormal protective mechanism to protect the victim from the recognition of the traumatic event (van der Kolk & Fisler, 1995). Although this dissociated state of consciousness initially serves a protective function, anesthetizing the victim from physical and psychological pain, the effects of a shattered "fight or flight" response are far-reaching and profound. Although dissociation may help to protect the victim from pain, it has the effect of making the victim more prone to ongoing victimization, precisely because the connection between the perpetrator and the pain he has inflicted has been blurred or severed. The victim is vulnerable to victimization not only by the initial perpetrator but by other individuals willing to capitalize on the victim's lack of a normal protective "fight or flight" response. The victim becomes an "easy mark."

For adolescent young women, and women in general, the violence of victimization is predominantly played out as sexual violation or rape, which by its nature produces psychological trauma. A study of rape survivors (Burgess & Holmstrom, 1974) found that every woman had symptoms of post-traumatic stress disorder in the immediate aftermath of the assault. The "dissolving" effects of trauma (Kardiner, 1947) on the normal system of self-protection, which impairs the victim's ability to react to threat, is compounded by another manifestation of the intrusive symptoms of post-traumatic stress disorder. This involves the reliving of the trauma in the form of reenactments—involuntary repetitions of some aspect of the trauma (Herman, 1997). Almost without exception, the person involved in the behavioral reenactment does not recognize the situation as a reenactment of the trauma (van der Kolk, 1989). The effect of reenactments is, once again, to put the victim at increased risk of further victimization by the initial perpetrator or subsequent perpetrators (van der Kolk & Fisler, 1993).

SEEKING AN EFFECTIVE RESPONSE

The traumatic effects of ongoing oppressive violence on victims renders them, to varying degrees, incapable of recognizing and responding rationally to coercive situations. Clearly, imposing a framework of rational decision making and skill building under these circumstances is wholly inadequate. Likewise, when the perpetrator is motivated by the desire to create a victim, he has already made a rational decision to choose techniques of coercion and control; he has already chosen the techniques precisely because of their utility to his goal attainment.

Given this reality, how does one respond to situations of coercion and oppression? When discussing oppressive violence at a *societal* level, Freire (1970) concludes that the answer lies in the process of recognizing and naming:

> The oppressed, who have been shaped by the death-affirming climate of oppression, must find through their struggle the way of life-affirming humanization. ... The oppressed have been destroyed precisely because their situation has reduced them to things. ... The struggle begins with men's [sic] *recognition* [emphasis added] that they have been destroyed. (p. 55)

Freire calls this process of recognition *conscientização*, or learning to perceive contradictions and take action against the oppressive elements of reality. *Conscientização* is a process of "naming"—of becoming aware (Freire, 1970). In this process, the oppressed become "*Subjects*—those who know and act, in contrast to *objects*, which are known and acted upon" (p. 20). The naming process on the societal level is mirrored on the interpersonal level; Herman (1997) describes the importance of "naming":

> Knowledge is power. ... No longer imprisoned in the wordlessness of the trauma, [the victim] discovers that there is a language for her experience. She discovers that she is not alone; others have suffered in similar ways. She discovers further that she is not crazy; the traumatic syndromes are normal human responses to extreme circumstances. And she discovers, finally, that she is not doomed to suffer this condition indefinitely; she can expect to recover, as others have recovered. (p. 158)

However, the effects of chronic trauma to the victim are not easy to transcend. Many victims never move from "victim" to "survivor" and never recognize the connection between their symptoms and their traumatic history. An essential element in the recovery process is telling the story of the trauma and integrating the traumatic memory into the survivor's life story. This process of recognition and naming, critical in the recovery process for the victim, is also critical for the field of conflict management if it aspires to effectively address the problem of violence occurring in victim–perpetrator relationships. A clear recognition and acknowledgment that the response to the violence of oppression must be different than the response to violence that arises from a lack of skill or impulse control is essential to avoid having conflict management and violence prevention practitioners revictimize the victim.

SEEKING EFFECTIVE PREVENTION

The violence of oppression in the form of domestic battery, rape, and child abuse is so prevalent that it is imperative that the field of conflict management come up with not only an effective response but a strategy for prevention. Once the field of conflict management has named the violence of oppression for what it is, a second step is to incorporate this definition of violence into conflict management and violence prevention training materials and curricula. Child and adolescent assault prevention programs have been doing this for more than a decade, and are a useful model. For example, the Child Assault Prevention program materials for adolescents (National Assault Prevention Center, 1986; Cooper, Lutter, & Phelps, 1983) focus on naming and clearly describing the types of behaviors that are coercive so that adolescents will recognize coercive control when they are confronted with it.

Child Assault Prevention (CAP) is an international child assault prevention program, headquartered in New Jersey, that offers developmentally appropriate educational programs in the schools for children and adolescents, including children with special needs. Prior to working with the youth, CAP facilitators conduct in-service workshops with school personnel and parents, stressing the point that assault prevention is the responsibility of the entire community—everyone is responsible for keeping children safe. CAP teaches children to recognize situations in which people are taking away their basic human rights to be "safe, strong, and free:"

> Safe is the right to feel okay—to not be scared—to not feel threatened or to be in danger. Strong is the right to feel good about yourself—to stand up for yourself—to feel that you can take care of yourself. Free is the right to make choices, particularly in regard to your own body. (CAP facilitator, personal communication, December 29, 1997)

CAP facilitators work with children to develop and practice strategies of self-assertion, peer support, and seeking the help of trusted adults. The TeenCAP program builds on the right to be "safe, strong, and free" by providing adolescents with an understanding of consent; force; neglect; emotional abuse; physical abuse; and sexual assault (forced sexual contact), including rape, incest, molestation, voyeurism, exhibitionism, pornography, and prostitution. Terms are defined in a straightforward and specific manner, eliminating a risk of misinterpretation; for example:

> *Consent:* Freely choosing to do something. Consent means you've said "yes," but you feel just as free to say *"no."*
> *Force:* Anything that prevents you from choosing freely to do something. Force can be emotional—"I'll commit suicide if you don't love me." It can be physical—"I'll hit you if you don't obey me." (*Safe, Strong & Free: A Guide for Teens*)

In the words of a CAP facilitator:

> All abuse is controlling people in different ways; CAP teaches how to recognize methods of control and presents strategies for recognizing and dealing with abuse.

CAP teaches that no one has the right to treat them in abusive ways, and that abuse is never their fault.

Assault prevention programs teach children and adolescents to recognize when people are taking away their rights, and respond to abusive situations. A discussion of dissociated coercion—the use of coercion in the context of a trusting relationship—can further illuminate this type of violence. Even when people recognize the warning signs of an abusive relationship, there is a sense of disbelief that violence could be occurring in one's own life—to reiterate, it doesn't "make sense" that a trusted individual would want to hurt you; it doesn't "fit."

Incorporating an awareness of the prevalence of violence-in-relationship, dissociated coercion, and the effects of interpersonal oppression into an understanding of the dynamics of conflict and violence is important for both practitioners and victims alike. My own experiences in presenting this information to students in class or training settings have been eye-opening. Without exception, I have encountered several individuals in each group (often the majority of the group) who have expressed to me that the description of dissociated coercion and the corresponding effects of trauma "are like looking in a mirror—I hear you describing myself."

For practitioners to begin to address the problem of oppressive interpersonal violence, conflict management and mediation trainers need first to acknowledge its existence and begin to incorporate an awareness of its effects into their practice. Without increased attention to the severe power imbalance inherent in oppression and coercive control, conflict management and violence prevention practitioners risk becoming passive perpetrators of the very violence they are seeking to control.

REFERENCES

Bureau of Justice Statistics. (1995). *Violence against women: Estimates from the redesigned survey.* August 1995, NCJ–154348.

Burgess, A. W., & Holmstrom, L. L. (1974). Rape trama syndrome. *American Journal of Psychiatry, 131,* 981–986.

Congressional Record Daily Edition. (1993, October 28). The Family Violence Prevention Act, p. H8640–8641.

Cooper, S., Lutter, Y., & Phelps, C. (1983). *Strategies for free children: A leader's guide to child assault prevention.* Columbus, OH: Child Assault Prevention Project, A Division of the National Assault Prevention Center.

Copeland, N. D. (1989). *Managing conflict: A curriculum for adolescents (Book 1).* Albuquerque, NM: New Mexico Center for Dispute Resolution.

Federal Bureau of Investigation. (1995). *Crime in the United States 1995: Uniform crime reports.*

Fisher, R., & Ury, W. L. (1981). *Getting to YES: Negotiating agreement without giving in.* Boston: Houghton Mifflin.

Freire, P. (1970). *Pedagogy of the oppressed* (M. B. Ramos, Trans.). New York: Seabury.

Hague, G., & Malos, E. (1993). *Domestic violence: Action for change.* Cleltenham, Great Britain: New Clarion.

Harvey, M. R., & Herman, J. L. (1994). Amnesia, partial amnesia, and delayed recall among adult survivors of childhood trauma. *Consciousness and Cognition, 4,* 295–306.

Herman, J. L. (1995). Crime and memory. *Bulletin of the American Academy of Psychiatry and the Law, 23,* 5–17.

Herman, J. L. (1997). *Trauma and recovery.* New York: Basic Books, HarperCollins.

Herman, J. L., & Schatzow, E. (1987). Recovery and verification of memories of childhood sexual trauma. *Psychoanalytic Psychology, 4,* 1–14.

Holmberg, M., & Halligan, J. (1992). *Conflict management for juvenile treatment facilities: A manual for training and program implementation* (1st ed.). San Francisco, CA: The Community Board Program, Inc.

Horowitz, M. (1986). *Stress response syndromes.* Northvale, NJ: Aronson.

Lax, D. A., & Sebenius, J. (1986). *The manager as negotiator.* New York: Free Press.

Maxwell, J. (1996). *Dissociated coercion.* Unpublished manuscript. Kent State University.

Metcalf, H. C. & Urwick, L. (Eds.). (1942). *Dynamic administration: The collected papers of Mary Parker Follett.* New York: Harper.

National Assault Prevention Center. (1986). *TeenCAP: An assault prevention curriculum committed to helping our teens stay safe, strong, and free.* Columbus, OH: National Assault Prevention Center.

Nietzsche, F. (1956). *The genealogy of morals* (F. Golffing, Trans.). New York: Anchor Books. (Original work published 1887)

Ohio Youth Services Network. (1993). *Keep yourself alive: A violence prevention curriculum.* Columbus: Ohio Youth Services Network.

Prothrow-Stith, D. (1987). *Violence prevention curriculum for adolescents.* Newton, MA: Education Development Center, Inc.

Rubin, J. Z. (1991). Some wise and mistaken assumptions about conflict and negotiation. In J. W. Breslin & J. Z. Rubin (Eds.), *Negotiation theory and practice.* Cambridge, MA: Program on Negotiation Books.

Russell, D. E. H. (1984). *Sexual exploitation: Rape, child sexual abuse, and sexual harassment.* Thousand Oaks, CA: Sage.

Sadalla, G., Henriquez, M., & Holmberg, M. (1987). *Conflict resolution: A secondary school curriculum.* San Francisco, CA: The Community Board Program, Inc.

Spiegel, D. (1989). Hypnosis in the treatment of victims of sexual abuse. *Psychiatric Clinics of North America, 12,* 295–305.

Susskind, L., & Cruickshank, J. (1987). *Breaking the impasse.* New York: Basic Books.

Ury, W. L. (1991). *Getting past no: Negotiating with difficult people.* New York: Bantam.

van der Kolk, B. A. (1989). The compulsion to repeat the trauma: Re-enactment, revictimization, and masochism. *Psychiatric Clinics of North America, 12,* 389–411.

van der Kolk, B. A., & Fisler, R. E. (1993). The biologic basis of posttraumatic stress. *Primary Care, 20,* 17–433.

van der Kolk, B. A., & Fisler, R. E. (1995). Dissociation and the fragmentary nature of traumatic memories: Overview and exploratory study. *Journal of Traumatic Stress, 8,* 505–525.

van der Kolk, B. A., MacFarlane, A. C., & Weisaeth, L. (Eds.), (1996). *Traumatic stress: The effects of overwhelming experience on mind, body, and society.* New York: Guilford.

Williams, L. M. (1994). Recall of childhood trauma: A prospective study of women's memories of child sexual abuse. *Journal of Consulting and Clinical Psychology, 62,* 1167–1176.

Williams, L. M. (1995). Recovered memories of abuse in women with documented child sexual victimization histories. *Journal of Traumatic Stress, 8,* 649–673.

Women's Action Coalition. (1993). *WAC Stats: Facts about women.* New York: The New Press.

PEACE AND CONFLICT: JOURNAL OF PEACE PSYCHOLOGY, 4(2), 167–178

The United Nations' Platform for Action: Critique and Implications

Susan R. McKay

Women's Studies
Univrsity of Wyoming

Deborah DuNann Winter

Department of Psychology
Whitman College

In August and September of 1995, the Fourth World Conference on Women was hosted in Beijing, China by the United Nations (UN). The gathering was the largest UN conference ever held, bringing together over 40,000 participants, including governmental representatives who attended the formal governmental conference and participants in the overlapping nongovernmental organizations (NGO) Forum in Huairou, China. The purpose of the official conference was to come to consensus concerning the final wording of the official policy document, the Platform for Action (PFA). One hundred and eighty-one member-nations signed the PFA, which committed them to the policies set forth there for improving the global status of women. In addition to focusing on women, the PFA gave much attention to peace. In this article, we present the peace agenda of the PFA, analyze the document's strengths, and limitations, and discuss the importance of incorporating its goals within the spheres of social action teaching, and research.

In September of 1995, China hosted the largest gathering for any United Nations (UN) conference ever held. Its purpose was to analyze and promote the status of women around the world. The Fourth World Conference on Women drew over 40,000 participants who attended one (or both) of two overlapping meetings: (a) the official governmental conference held in Beijing, attended by 6,000 governmental representatives from 181 member nations, 4,000 representatives of accredited non-

Requests for reprints should be sent to Susan R. McKay, Women's Studies, University of Wyoming, P.O. Box 4297, Laramie, WY 82071–3065. E-Mail: mckay@uwyo.edu

governmental organizations, and approximately 4,000 media representatives and civil servants; and (b) the nongovernmental organizations (NGO) conference, which preceded the governmental conference by 7 days and overlapped it for 3 days, held 35 miles from Beijing in Huairou, and attended by over 30,000 women, men, and youth.[1]

This conference on the global status of women followed three before it. The first, held in Mexico City in 1975, initiated the United Nations (UN) Decade for Women 1975–1985. A mid-decade meeting in Copenhagen followed, and a third conference in Nairobi in 1985 closed the decade. The purpose of this fourth meeting, held a decade after "the decade," was to assess progress made on women's issues since the Decade for Women and craft a set of observable, public commitments to be made by member governments for improving the status of women. These public commitments are widely distributed through the document that emerged from the conference, named The UN Platform for Action (hereafter called PFA; United Nations, 1996).

Whereas the governmental conference was convened primarily to arrive at consensus about the final wording of the official PFA, the NGO forum in Huairou focused more broadly on women's global concerns, networking for activism, and lobbying governmental representatives in order to influence the final wording of the PFA. NGOs have played a powerful role in affecting UN conference outcomes. In the words of First Lady Hillary Rodham Clinton, "Time and time again we have seen that it is NGOs that are responsible for making progress in any society. ... It is the NGOs that have pressured governments and have led governments down the path to economic, social, and political progress, often in the face of overwhelming hostility" (Clinton, 1996). As in other UN world conferences, NGOs played an important role in affecting the final wording of the PFA.

Due in part to the hard work of many NGOs, peace issues received important attention in the PFA. We begin by describing the format of the PFA, discussing the peace-related portions of it. We then indicate the curious paradox between the document's many impressive statements emphasizing the importance of achieving global peace and the lack of specific measurable actions crafted to achieve it. We also address the U.S. national agenda derived from the PFA and its almost total silence about peace issues. Finally, we offer a hypothesis about why action strategies for working towards peace received such limited treatment in the PFA. We then discuss implications for teaching and research.

---

[1]The authors joined Eileen Borris, Faye Campbell, and Anne Cowardin-Bach, as a group of Division 48 and Psychologists for Social Responsibility members, to participate under the auspices of Psychologists for Social Responsibility and Women for Meaningful Summits, at the nongovernmental organizations (NGO) conference.

THE UN PLATFORM FOR ACTION (PFA)

The intent of the world conference was to come to consensus about the final wording of a document that was comprehensive in scope but manageable in size. The document evolved after several years of discussion and preparation, at community, regional, national, and eventually world regional meetings, involving multiple conferences of both governmental and NGO participants. Going into the final Beijing meeting, 40% of the PFA was bracketed, meaning that consensus on particular phrases had not been achieved in the numerous preliminary meetings. The final version of the PFA was adopted by the Fourth World Conference on Women on September 15, 1995 after much last minute negotiation and compromise.

The Beijing Declaration

Peace has a strong emphasis in this part of the document. For example, the preamble expresses the determination "to advance the goals of equality, development and peace for all women everywhere" (UN, 1996, Para. 3, p. 7). Several forceful statements affirm the possibility of a peaceful world and recognize women's peacebuilding capacities for creating it, for example, "local, national, regional and global peace is attainable and is inextricably linked with the advancement of women, who are a fundamental force for leadership, conflict resolution and the promotion of lasting peace at all levels" (Para. 18, p. 8). Later, the Preamble promises that governments will

> take positive steps to ensure peace for the advancement of women, and, recognizing the leading role that women have played in the peace movement, work actively towards general and complete disarmament under strict and effective international control, and support negotiations on the conclusion, without delay, of a universal and multilaterally and effectively verifiable comprehensive nuclear-test-ban treaty that contributes to nuclear disarmament and the prevention of the proliferation of nuclear weapons in all of its aspects. (UN, 1996, Para. 28, p. 9)

The declaration does not use the term "peacebuilding" per se, but it explicitly cites peacebuilding activities, such as eradicating poverty, addressing the structural causes of poverty through changes in economic structures, and promoting sustainable development—processes that peace psychologists recognize as those contributing to the development of positive peace.

Chapter 1: Mission Statement

The Mission Statement also stresses the importance of achieving peace: the "PFA requires immediate and concerted action by all to create a peaceful, just and humane world" (Para. 4, p. 17–18). No document from the previous three global women's conferences has emphasized so strongly the shared partnership of men and women in achieving peace as does the PFA:

> Equality between women and men is a matter of human rights and a condition for social justice and is also a necessary and fundamental prerequisite for equality, development and peace. A transformed partnership based on equality between women and men is a condition for people-centered sustainable development. A sustained and long-term commitment is essential so that women and men can work together for themselves, for their children and for society to meet the challenges of the twenty-first century. (Para. 1, p. 17)

Chapter 2: Global Framework

This section again explicitly affirms the importance of women in achieving peace:

> Recognizing that the achievement and maintenance of peace and security are a precondition for economic and social progress, women are increasingly establishing themselves as central actors in a variety of capacities in the movement of humanity for peace. Their full participation in decision-making, conflict prevention and resolution and all other peace initiatives is essential to the realization of lasting peace. (Para. 23, p. 25)

The links between peace and the status of women are further emphasized by the statement that

> the maintenance of peace and security at the global, regional, and local levels, together with the prevention of policies of aggression and ethnic cleansing and the resolution of armed conflict, is crucial for the protection of the human rights of women and girl-children, as well as for the elimination of all forms of violence against them and of their use as a weapon of war. (Para. 12, pp. 22–23)

Finally, this chapter articulates the negative relation between militarism and social development by discussing the corrosive effects of military budgets on the well-being of citizens. In its words, "excessive military expenditures and arms trade or trafficking, and investments for arms production and acquisition have reduced the resources available for social development" (Para. 13, p. 23). The statement goes on to criticize structural adjustment policies by pointing out that they punish the poorest citizens, who are always disproportionately women. Also contributing to the global feminization of poverty is environmental degradation that affects all humanity but "often has a more direct impact on women" (Para. 34, p. 28). It adds that, in order to be successful, the search for people-centered sustainable development must involve women.

Chapter 3: Critical Areas of Concern

Noting that "most of the goals set out in the Nairobi Forward-Looking Strategies for the Advancement of Women have not been achieved" (Para. 42, p. 33), this chapter mentions "wars of aggression, armed conflicts, colonial or other forms of alien domination or foreign occupation, civil wars and terrorism" (Para. 42, p. 33) as the most important barriers to women's empowerment. The chapter then enumerates the 12 critical areas of concern that the body of the PFA examines more closely.

Chapter 4: Strategic Objectives and Actions

The essence of the PFA is contained in chapter 4, which details the 12 concerns and concrete actions to be taken to remedy each concern. Although all of the critical concerns in the PFA must be addressed for world peace, because all speak to the interlinked goals of peace, development, and equality, we will focus on the strategic objectives that are most closely aligned with concerns of peace psychologists. These objectives are contained in Section E: Women and Armed Conflict, which discusses the multiple ways armed conflict adversely impacts women and girls.

The section begins by reiterating that, in order for the advancement of women to occur, an environment that maintains world peace and promotes and protects human rights, democracy, and the peaceful settlement of disputes is necessary; that cooperative approaches to peace and security are urgently needed; and that equal access and full participation of women in power structures and in all efforts is necessary for the prevention and resolution of conflicts (Para. 131–135, pp. 82–84).

The effects of armed conflict are described as particularly salient for women and girls because of their lower status and their sex (Para. 136, p. 84). For example, 80% of the world's millions of refugees and other displaced persons are women and children, and they suffer from multiple deprivations and humiliations, including sexual violence (Para. 136, p. 84). Also, "many women's non-governmental organizations have called for reductions in military expenditures worldwide, as well as in international trade and trafficking in and the proliferation of weapons" (Para. 138, p. 85), from which most negative effects are experienced by people living in poverty. Furthermore, with " ... more than 100 million anti-personnel land mines scattered in 64 countries" (Para. 137, p. 85), rural women living in poverty especially suffer from arms' indiscriminate effects because women work the land and are usually the fuel and water gatherers for their families.

During times of armed conflict, women's roles are crucial, as the collapse of communities require that they enlist in preserving the social order (Para. 139, p. 85). The PFA cites the role of women in creating a culture of peace by noting that "women make an important but often unrecognized contribution as peace educators both in their families and in their societies" (Para. 139, p. 85).

Finally, and of central importance, the section states that "education to foster a culture of peace that upholds justice and tolerance for all nations and peoples is essential to attaining lasting peace and should be begun at an early age. It should include elements of conflict resolution, mediation, reduction of prejudice, and respect for diversity" (Para. 140, p. 85). Programs and policies addressing armed and other conflicts should have a highly visible gender perspective mainstreamed into all discussions.

The document then lists five Strategic Objectives concerning women and armed conflict that are designed to address the problems enumerated previously:

Strategic Objective E.1 Increase the participation of women in conflict resolution at decision-making levels and protect women living in situations of armed and other conflicts or under foreign occupation (p. 85). Among the actions to be taken are creating equal participation of women in all forums and peace activities at all levels, including the UN; integrating a gender perspective in the resolution of armed or other conflicts and foreign occupation; using gender balance in nominating or promoting candidates for judicial and other positions in all relevant international bodies; and ensuring these bodies are able to address gender issues properly by providing appropriate training to prosecutors, judges, and other officials who are handling gender-sensitive cases.

Strategic Objective E.2 Reduce excessive military expenditures and control the availability of armaments (p. 86). Actions identified under this objective focus on military conversion; reducing excessive military expenditures and trade in arms; and achieving global agreements to stop the production, export, and use of antipersonnel land mines and reduce their damaging effects. This section also promises to

> work actively towards general and complete disarmament under strict and effective international control; support negotiations on the conclusion, without delay, of a universal and multilaterally and effectively verifiable comprehensive nuclear test ban treaty that contributes to nuclear disarmament and the prevention of the proliferation of nuclear weapons in all its aspects. (Para. f.i.ii, p. 87)

Strategic Objective E.3 Promote nonviolent forms of conflict resolution and reduce the incidence of human rights abuse in conflict situations (p. 88). To accomplish this objective, governments agreed to ratify international agreements related to the protection of women and children in armed conflicts, respect humanitarian law in armed conflicts, and advance women's representation at all decision-making levels in national and international institutions. Of particular interest to peace psychologists is a recommendation on preventing violence against women: that there be gender-sensitive concerns in developing training programs for all relevant personnel on international humanitarian law and human rights awareness, including those involved in the UN peace-keeping and humanitarian aid missions.

Strategic Objective E.4 Promote women's contributions to fostering a culture of peace (p. 90). Actions to be taken include promoting peaceful conflict resolution, reconciliation, and tolerance; conducting peace research involving the participation of women; examining the impact of armed conflict on women and children; increasing women's contributions to peace movements; establishing innovative mechanisms for containing violence and for conflict resolution; and developing educational programs for boys and girls to foster a culture of peace.

Strategic Objective E.5 Provide protection, assistance, and training to refugee women, other displaced women in need of international protection, and internally displaced women (p. 90). Among the multiple actions recommended are that women be involved in the planning, design, implementation, monitoring, and evaluation of programs for refugee and other internally displaced women; that the rights, safety, and rehabilitation of refugee women be addressed; and that the international community cooperate in addressing the problems of refugee women and children.

THE PFA'S AMBIVALENT COMMITMENT TO PEACE

Clearly, the PFA makes numerous and cogent statements about global peace and its interlinked relations with structural factors, such as social development, gender equality, environmental restoration, and respect for human rights. The language of the PFA was hard-won, a result of heroic lobbying efforts by international leadership from NGOs and government leaders alike. The PFA has been applauded for its discussion of peace. In the words of feminist Robin Morgan (1996):

> This is a document that criticizes structural adjustment programs; advises cuts in military spending in favor of social spending; urges women's participation at all peace talks and in all decision making that affects development planning and environment issues; confronts violence against women—and specifies that sexual harassment, battery, dowry attacks, female genital mutilation, and rape (as well as rape as a war crime) are violations of human rights. (p. 81)

However, Morgan also notes that "there are precious few time lines" (p. 81). One of the major flaws of the document is that it rarely states goals in observable measurable terms. There are only a handful of statements in the document that offer observable measurable goals to be completed by specified dates. One example of a clear time line is Strategic objective B.1: Ensure equal access to education, which specifies that

> By the year 2000, provide universal access to basic education and ensure completion of primary education by at least 80 per cent of primary school-age children; close the gender gap in primary and secondary school education by the year 2005; provide universal primary education in all countries before the year 2015. (Para. 80.b, p. 49)

In other words, countries were able to agree to specified goals with explicit time lines for education. Similarly, they were able to do it for health care. Consider Strategic objective C.1: Increase women's access throughout the life cycle to appropriate, affordable and quality health care, information, and related services:

> Reduce ill health and maternal morbidity and achieve worldwide the agreed-upon goal of reducing maternal mortality by at least 50 per cent of the 1990 levels by the year 2000 and a further one half by the year 2025; ensure that the necessary services are available at each level of the health system and make reproductive health care accessible, through the primary health-care system, to all individuals of appropriate ages as soon as possible and no later than the year 2015. (Para. 106.i, p. 63)

Likewise, countries were able to agree to specifiable time lines for integrating women into decision making in general (Para. 182, p. 109), and in the UN in particular (Para. 193.c, p. 114); ratifying the Convention on the Elimination of all Forms of Violence Against Women (CEDAW) by the year 2000 (Para. 230.b, p. 126); implementing The Convention on the Rights of the Child by the year 2000 (Para. 230.l, p. 127; para 274.a, p. 148); and providing universal safe drinking water by the year 2000 (Para. 256.l, p. 143).

However, no such time lines were given for armed conflict despite numerous calls made in the preparatory meetings by many NGOs for a 5% reduction in global military expenditures a year for the next 10 years, achieving a 50% reduction by the year 2005. Generic language about arms reduction remained but specific goals were deleted. It is paradoxical that the achievement of peace, such a central goal of the UN and of the rhetoric of the PFA, had no analogous time lines in the section on Armed Conflict. The one and only strategic objective that does mention a time line is found in paragraph 143.e (p. 87) that promises to "work toward" (rather than achieve) prohibition of land mines:

> Undertake to work actively towards ratification, if they have not already done so, of the 1981 Convention on Prohibitions or Restrictions on the Use of Certain Conventional Weapons Which May Be Deemed to Be Excessively Injurious or to Have Indiscriminate Effects, particularly the Protocol on Prohibitions or Restrictions on the Use of Mines, Booby Traps and Other Devices (Protocol II, 26) with a view to universal ratification by the year 2000.

No specified goals are given for conversion of military spending, increasing women's roles in conflict resolution, promoting nonviolent forms of conflict resolution and reducing the incidence of human rights abuse in conflict situations; promoting women's contribution to fostering a culture of peace; providing protection, assistance, and training to refugee women, other displaced women in need of international protection, and internally displaced women; or providing assistance to the women of the colonies and nonself-governing territories, all of which are objectives of the PFA. For these reasons, the PFA shows a curious paradox: Although there is ample and inspired articulation of the importance and achievability of world peace throughout the document, there is little in the strategic objectives to hold governments to measurable commitments.

THE U.S. RESPONSE: PEACE VIRTUALLY DISAPPEARS

Like all participating countries, the United States derived its own set of national priorities from the PFA: in this case, under the auspices of the President's Interagency Council on Women. In a document dated June 13, 1996 the Council asked for citizen responses to six areas, one of which was called SECURITY, and included issues of

> domestic violence, rape, sexual harassment, violent crime, gun control, safety, law enforcement, the judicial system, prisons, conflict resolution, diplomacy, peacemaking, peacekeeping, weapons, war, violence in the media (President's Interagency Council on Women, 1996, p. 3).

Responding to this request, Psychologists for Social Responsibility's national coordinator submitted a briefing paper entitled "Improving our capacity for nonviolent conflict resolution: A long-term strategy for implementation of the Platform for Action" (Anderson, 1996), which urged the Council to highlight nonviolent conflict resolution training in its response to the PFA. However, the Council's September, 1996 paper entitled "U.S. Government Follow-up to the UN World Conference on Women: September, 1996: Update on Key Initiatives" made no mention of conflict resolution or nonviolence training, and it did not mention peacemaking or peacekeeping, weapons, war, or violence in the media. The document does describe an effort to "fight domestic and other forms of violence by combining tough Federal laws with the state and local assistance in law enforcement, victim assistance, prosecutions and crime prevention" (President's Interagency Council on Women, 1996, p. 3).

These initiatives include a national Domestic Violence Hotline and a grant program to combat domestic violence. The document also states that ratification of the Convention of the Elimination of all Forms of Violence Against Women is a top priority among international treaties. These actions fall very short of the vision of peacebuilding in the PFA. Highlighting the problem of violence against women is important, but focusing entirely on it as a peace issue promotes the image of women only as victims, rather than as powerful peacemakers and peacebuilders in their communities and national governments.

Similarly the widely publicized White House Follow-up Teleconference broadcast on September 28, 1996, which was to focus on the U.S. response to the PFA, gave no attention to any peace issues other than mentioning the Domestic Violence Hotline. The White House has shown leadership addressing domestic violence, which has been defined as a crime in the U.S. only since 1977. But a Domestic Violence Hotline in no way approaches the larger and more important conception of peacebuilding that saturates the Platform for Action. More specifically, the U.S. response, via the White House Interagency Council, has no current discussion of conflict resolution, arms control, land mines, military conversion, women as peacebuilders, or cultures of peace, which are all key elements of the PFA strategies for facilitating peace.

THE ABANDONMENT OF PEACE

Why did the United States ignore peace issues in its response to the PFA? There are several possibilities, including the cynical view that the White House had little interest in promoting the welfare of women beyond ensuring women's vote in the upcoming Presidential election (which followed the Follow-up Teleconference by only 6 weeks). Because the United States was not at war, peace was not an election topic. However, domestic violence was, through the widely publicized O.J. Simpson murder trial the previous year, which made domestic violence an election issue. Furthermore, the American public is not familiar with the notion of peacebuilding, for example, the idea that peace must be structurally approached by working towards the achievement of sustainable development, gender equality, environmental protection, and protection of human rights.

Why would a document so frequently and effectively proclaim the importance of global peace and then not make specific commitments for achieving it? One explanation is that gender bias permits women to lobby successfully for some issues but not others. Women can successfully engage in discussions of health care, education, even water supplies, and push their governments toward specifiable goals in connection with these traditionally "women's issues". However, matters of "national security"—arms trade, military expenditures, military conversion, who gets to negotiate the end of wars and on what terms— are usually matters for men. In the words of one arms control observer,

> All of the arms reduction measures for Beijing were axed at the regional governmental meetings—swiftly and without the involvement of NGOs....The Beijing Conference was somewhat remarkable in that the preparatory process allowed for the participation of women on a number of different levels—grassroots/NGO, regional, national, etc. By contrast, international decision making on arms control issues takes place in forums where there is relatively little access (treaty conferences, the Conference on Disarmament, the UN First Committee). [Because women don't participate in these meetings] "peace as a women's issue" is not yet mainstream (J. McKay, personal communication, November 23, 1996).

Perhaps it is unrealistic to expect that a UN document would push hard for reduction of global military spending considering that 4 of the 5 permanent members of the Security Council supply 80% of the world's arms trade (Christie, 1997).

Implications for Social Action

Women and men all over the world will need to continue to pressure their governments to pursue peacebuilding, reducing arms expenditures that directly detract from social development, and highlight the importance of building cultures of peace as a matter of "national security" in the 21st century. This means that women's perspectives must be integrated into decisions made about militarization and arms expenditures. The UN (1996) *Platform for Action* made a good case for peacebuilding, but governments will have to change how they operate in order to actualize its vision.

Clinicians and activists will find important guidance within the PFA for action on behalf of women from community to international levels. Because this is a global document, a goodly proportion of the strategies require local work no matter where one lives. In the United States, there have been state-wide coalitions that have gathered to identify priorities for their specific geographic areas and to develop action plans based upon these areas. Because the peace platform of the U.S. agenda is diluted, it seems especially important that peace psychologists be active in bringing this to the forefront both in terms of local and national policy. Outside of the United States, psychologists can find out what national priorities have been established and also work for increased integration of strategies that encourage peacebuilding. Such action is already occurring in Canada where specific policy recommendations have been submitted to integrate gender into Canadian initiatives on peacebuilding. There are also strategies that require activism by psychologists wherever they live—for example, in working for disarmament, the banning of antipersonnel mines, and reduction in military expenditures.

Implications for Teaching and Research

Psychologists should find many areas of application to teaching and research. The contents of the PFA are not subject to copyright so it can be reproduced for widespread use. Information can be obtained through the UN Department of Public Information, Room S–1005, United Nations Headquarters, New York, NY 10017, FAX 212 963 4556. Relevant sections of the document can be copied for use in teaching, to highlight global concerns of women and girls and specific areas of concern (for example, armed conflict, human rights, education of the girl child, the environment, violence against women, women and health, conflict resolution, and women and decision making). Susan McKay has used sections of the document in several classes, including courses on leadership, women's health, and women and war. Students have initially responded with skepticism that the stated goals and strategies are achievable; with increasing discussion and student implementation of community-based projects derived directly from the PFA strategies, students begin to feel empowered by their ability to act to make a difference and they better understand the effectiveness of collective individual initiatives in making change. For example, students worked directly from PFA strategies to improve campus lighting, involve more women voters in the issues for the 1996 elections, and to educate the public about the effects of welfare reform upon university women.

For researchers, the PFA is a document of opportunities. Although the PFA contains a substantial amount of written material related to women and peace, there needs to be much greater focus on research about women's roles in peacemaking and peacebuilding. How do women "do" conflict resolution? Do their approaches differ from men's ? How are women impacted by war, and what psychological approaches are effective in healing wounds both at individual and community levels? What are ways to increase women's capabilities and capacities in peace-making and peacebuilding? What are women's cross-cultural differences and similarities with respect to peacemaking and peacebuilding activities? Literally every section of the PFA provides opportunities for the generation of important research questions for peace psychologists.

Despite limitations, the PFA is a blueprint for political action and scholarship on behalf of girls and women thoughout the world. Whether through teaching, activism, research, or all of them, bringing the agenda of the PFA to actuality is critically important in the effort to achieve a more peaceful and just world.

REFERENCES

Anderson, A. (1996). *Improving our capacity for nonviolent conflict resolution: A long-term strategy for implementation of the Platform for Action Signed at the UN Fourth World Conference on Women, Beijing, Sept. 4–15, 1996.* (Briefing paper available from Psychologists for Social Responsibility, 2607 Connecticut Ave. NW, Washington, DC 20008)

Clinton, H. R. (1996). Words to break the silence: Excerpts, remarks to the NGO Forum, 6 September 1995. *Women's Studies Quarterly, 23* (1 & 2), 42–45.

Christie, D. (1996). Reducing direct and structural violence: the human needs theory. *Peace and Conflict: Journal of Peace Psychology, 3,* 315–332.

Morgan, R. (1996). The UN Conference: Out of the holy brackets and into the policy mainstream. *Women's Studies Quarterly, 23* (1 & 2), 77–83.

President's Interagency Council on Women. (1995). *U.S. Government follow-up to the U.N. World Conference on Women: September 1996 update on key 26 initiatives.* (Available from The White House: New Executive Office Building, Suite 3212, Washington, DC 20503)

President's Interagency Council on Women. (1996). *Towards a National Action Agenda. June 13, 1996.* (Available from The White House: New Executive Office Building, Suite 3212, Washington, DC 20503)

United Nations. (1996). *The Platform for Action and the Beijing Declaration.* New York: United Nations Department of Public Information.

PEACE AND CONFLICT: JOURNAL OF PEACE PSYCHOLOGY, 4(2), 179–180

Transforming Conflict

David Riches

Department of Social Anthropology
University of St. Andrews, Scotland

This book focuses on the quandary of Western academic experts in the social sciences. In business, because of the existence of "social problems," such experts all too often propose solutions discrepant with the cultural assumptions of the people they are summoned to help. In addition, such "recipients" need not necessarily be members of a nonwestern society; equally, they could be from the working classes in, say, Europe or America. This book discusses this state of affairs with regard to the important matter of conflict resolution, with Western peacemakers purveying their expertise in such places as Central America and Africa providing the main illustrations. By and large, in its practical recommendations, the book resolves the experts' quandary in a satisfying way.

The book, which consists of a relatively acceptable mixture of abstract modelling, anecdotal field examples and practical recommendations, focuses on the training of local people as conflict resolvers in a variety of social and cultural settings. Its main concern is to draw out what the author calls the eliciting dimension in such training. Such a dimension recognises the trainees' culture not just as something the Western expert must "take into account" but rather as the key resource in terms of which locally empowering methods of conflict resolution may be established. In elicitation, the expert functions not as a provider of ready-made recipes for peace but instead as a facilitator, whose task is to draw out, and build on, already existing indigenous wisdom. Indeed, local culture may provide the very basis for the societal restructurings, or transformations, which the outside expert, desiring to maximise the beneficial implications of conflict, seeks to bring about.

The book's anthropologically sensitive emphasis on the trainees' culture raises the question of whether the Western expert might be dispensed with altogether. The

---

Preparing for Peace: Conflict Transformation across Cultures, John Paul Lederach, 1995, Syracuse, NY: Syracuse University Press.

Requests for reprints should be sent to David Riches, Department of Social Anthropology, University of St. Andrews, Fife, Scotland KY16 9AL.

author insists that a measure of professional guidance is going to be necessary in any instance of conflict resolution and theorizes the point by arguing that the framing of conflict resolution is built on universalistic assumptions. Thus, although strategy and tactics relating to a particular instance of conflict should capitalize on what the local culture provides, such "functional" matters as the importance of locating mutually acceptable third parties will hold good in all settings. This is well illustrated when the author draws a contrast between conflict resolution relating to U.S. communities and that relating to Somali communities. In both instances, mediators will operate within a common framework of what conflict resolution is all about, but, when it comes to practical returns, success in the former relies on relatively individualistic and bureaucratic procedures, whereas success in the latter will come through working through interclan councils and through recognising the culturally significant web of ongoing relationships in which every person is suspended. To underscore his argument, the author might, at this point, have mentioned the United States' recent disastrous peacemaking efforts in Somalia.

This book is a courageous discourse on conflict resolution in that it insists, following Adam Curle, that matters of justice, requiring restructuring in favour of the less powerful, must always inform the peacemaking process. Here, the tension between the recipient's culture and the value-judgements of the Western expert is the most exposed. According to the author, much injustice is "covert": Local people may barely be aware of it, and the outside professional has first to bring it fully into people's consciousness. It is a pity that this nonnegotiable assertion is not really illustrated in any of the examples the author provides in the second half of the book. After all, what is injustice to the culturally democratic Western expert may be culturally entirely proper to local people. For example, implicit in the author's position is that the status of women that obtains in many developing countries is an appropriate concern for Western conflict resolvers.

In the event, whenever Westerners provide expertise to other cultures, contradictions relating to their respective positions can never totally be avoided. The merit of this book is that, relating to the arena of peacemaking, it combines relatively successful levels of both practical recommendation and anthropological sensitivity. Given the intractable topic, it is probably as good as one could possibly expect.

PEACE AND CONFLICT: JOURNAL OF PEACE PSYCHOLOGY, 4(2), 181–182

West Side Story Revisited

Janet R. Brice-Baker

Ferkauf Graduate School of Psychology
Yeshiva University

Clinical Interventions with Gang Adolescents and their Families by Curtis W. Branch makes a significant and influential contribution to many areas of knowledge. It is an appropriate volume for reading by professionals in the clinical psychology, clinical social work, psychiatric, psychiatric nursing, legal, and correctional fields. In many ways, this book serves as a tutorial on the gang subculture.

It is divided into three major sections: theory and foundations, clinical assessment, and interventions. The first section includes discussions on such topics as the history of gangs, the developmental aspects of gang membership, and race and ethnicity as factors to consider in gang membership and gang loyalty and how gangs fit into their respective ethnic and racial communities. Chapters 4–8 comprise the second part. Dr. Branch recommends a five-part assessment consisting of the mental status examination, behavioral assessment, cognitive assessment, family assessment, and developmental assessment. Although none of the aforementioned areas is new to the trained clinician, this portion of the book points out those aspects of living in and around gangs that uniquely influence an assessment. The third part of the book instructs didactically and through illustration how to plan and execute an intervention with a gang adolescent and his or her family, once he or she is engaged in treatment.

The undergirding theme of the book challenges stereotypes about gangs. The author points out that these stereotypes are not only well known but well documented by the print and visual media. Such mediums take a canvas and paint a portrait of gang members in vivid hues of poverty, violence, and illiteracy. Gangs become the embodiment of what we fear the most and, in some cases, that fear is

---

Clinical Interventions with Gang Adolescents and their Families, Curtis W. Branch, 1997, Boulder, CO: Westview.

Requests for reprints should be sent to Janet R. Brice-Baker, Yeshiva University, Ferkauf Graduate School of Psychology, Albert Einstein College of Medicine Campus, 1300 Morris Park Avenue, Rousso Building, 3rd Floor, Bronx, NY 10461.

projected onto certain racial groups. Branch points out that "gangs are not relegated to one class, race, or ethnic group." He suggests that the challenge to working clinically with this population lies not just in the streets but in our fear and ignorance. Before any type of treatment program can be developed, funded, and set in place, we as mental health professionals must scrutinize out motivation for working with gang members.

Research, even empirical research, has not been foolproof in providing society (and in this particular case the mental health field) with answers to our myriad questions about gang adolescents. The author states that the reasons for these failures are manifold. First, research is not divorced from the individuals conducting it. This means that what we decide to research, how we formulate our hypotheses, our sampling procedures, and interpretation of findings may all be influenced by preconceived notions of gangs. A perfect example of our bias exists in the use of the term *gang*. It suggests a homogenous, undifferentiated mass. Perhaps the author is attempting to individualize the membership when he uses the term *gang adolescent* in the title. Another failure of researchers has been their concentration on the area of gang members and violence to the exclusion of other issues. Branch's review of the literature suggests that there is nothing on the premorbid personality of the gang member and no research on the structure and organization of gangs. Gangs seem to be studied in isolation with emphasis on their ethnic make-up (which has not yielded any useful information), their criminal activities, or both. It is as if the teenagers who comprise the gangs spring up in society out of thin air.

A major and possibly the most important contribution of this book is the author's systemic analysis of the adolescent gang member. He considers the adolescent's family environment, school environment, neighborhood environment, and peer group. The text is rich in clinical case material and step-by-step instructions for a Family Intervention Project (FIP).

In an era of escalating violence between countries and escalating violence within the United States, people are becoming more frightened of their fellow humans. Within that gestalt is a piece that points to increased fear regarding the violence of youth in this country—much of youth violence is attributed to gangs. Branch leaves us with several questions: Can gang adolescents resolve the conflict within themselves? What part can psychologists play in the healing of the gang-affiliated adolescent, his or her community, and the larger public?

PEACE AND CONFLICT: JOURNAL OF PEACE PSYCHOLOGY, 4(2), 183–185

United States Imperialism, Nuclear Threats, and the Voices of the *Hibakusha*

Eric Herring

Department of Politics
University of Bristol

Illustrated with analyses of U.S. nuclear weapons policy regarding Hiroshima and Nagasaki, the Cuban missile crisis, Vietnam, and the Middle East, Joseph Gerson argues that the abolition of nuclear weapons is a continuing imperative. His main subthemes are as follows:

- Nuclear weapons have been used to maintain the U.S. "empire" and its "spheres of influence:" They were only secondarily acquired to pursue the Cold War with the Soviet Union.
- The Vietnam War was "the logical extension of centuries of U.S. foreign military intervention" (p. xii).
- The United States has been prepared to use subversion, military intervention, and nuclear threats to "gain and regain" control of oil in the Middle East.
- The U.S. peace movement has, on the whole, failed to address properly the issues of intervention, justice, and peace regarding the Palestinian–Israeli conflict due to racism.
- The use of nuclear threats by the United States "has encouraged and, within the game of nations, legitimized its imitation by other nations unwilling to accept the discriminatory nuclear order codified in the non-proliferation regime" (p. xviii).

With Hiroshima Eyes. Atomic War, Nuclear Extortion and Moral Imagination, 1995, Joseph Gerson, Philadelphia: New Society Publishers. [Published in cooperation with American Friends Service Committee, New England Regional Office.]

Requests for reprints should be sent to Eric Herring, Department of Politics, University of Bristol, 10 Priory Road, Bristol BS8 1TU, England. E-mail: eric.herring@bristol.ac.uk

- "For most Americans, even those engaged in the peace and nuclear disar-mament movements, the victims of the atomic bombings of Hiroshima and Nagasaki are abstractions, marginalized *others*" (p. xiii).
- The *hibakusha*—the survivors of the atomic bombings of Hiroshima and Nagasaki—have something important to contribute to our understanding of nuclear weapons.

With its polemical and emotive style, this book may reinvigorate the converted and mobilize some who had not previously taken a strong line. However, the book will be dismissed by those who see some level of nuclear armament as an important and legitimate element of U.S. security policy.

Authors, such as McGeorge Bundy, Richard Betts, Richard Ned Lebow, and Janice Stein have given us historical research of very high quality on the use of nuclear threats by the United States. The four case study chapters that form the core of the book contain little that is original, and there is almost no use of primary materials. Gerson does not help his credibility as a historian by consistently misspelling "Khrushchev" as "Khruschev." What Gerson does is to steep the cases in moral condemnation of U.S. policy. The argument that the United States has been and continues to be an imperial power has been articulated most clearly by writers such as Noam Chomsky and Edward Herman. Gerson adds to that literature by linking the nuclear threats literature to the U.S.-as-empire literature.

The claim that the hibakusha have something important to say about nuclear weapons is, at one level, something with which virtually everyone would agree: The hibakusha remind us that nuclear weapons can inflict horrific suffering. The point has been articulated well before by Freeman Dyson (1984), who argued in his book *Weapons and Hope* that we need to supplement the voices of the nuclear warriors with the voices of the nuclear victims. Beyond the general claim that the hibakusha deserve a deeply respectful hearing, Gerson is unclear in both his claims and the evidence to support them. He asserts that, "among many people in Japan and the United States there is, I fear, … a dehumanizing belief that the hibakusha have nothing to share but their pain" (p. 7). He does not explain why that reasonable and plausible (though, of course, not necessarily right) perspective is either dehu-manizing or wrong. He claims that, "for years, hibakusha have complained that the media's descriptions of the holocausts of Hiroshima and Nagasaki do not begin to communicate what they endured and saw" (p. xv). However, he does not elaborate on this. The Japanese Confederation of Organizations of Atomic and Hydrogen Bombs Sufferers seeks the abolition of nuclear weapons. It condemns the way that the United States has sought to prevent North Korea from acquiring nuclear weapons while reserving for itself the right to retain and even initiate the use of nuclear weapons if it deems it necessary. This is a legitimate criticism of apparent double standards, but one does not have to be a hibakusha to arrive at that position. Gerson fleetingly draws a parallel between the hibakusha and the survivors of the

Nazi Judeocide (p. 8). However, many of the survivors of the Judeocide have ended up advocating the opposite position from the hibakusha—namely that their suffering gives them the right to acquire nuclear weapons and to use extreme measures in order to protect themselves. Gerson does not explore this stark contrast.

All in all, Gerson's book takes some steps in an important direction, namely, encouraging people to listen to the hibakusha. However, it is something of a missed opportunity and a frustrating read due to the failure to clearly articulate any kind of disciplined research design. If he had done so, the reader could have understood the hibakusha much more clearly.

The earth's human beings are running out of available resources, polluting our natural habitat, and reproducing too quickly. Yet we proceed to live as if our normal lives will continue.

Deborah DuNann Winter, 1996

PEACE AND CONFLICT: JOURNAL OF PEACE PSYCHOLOGY, 4(2), 187–189

Interactive Conflict Resolution: The Last 30 Years and Beyond

Kevin Avruch

Department of Sociology and Anthropology,
George Mason University

By "interactive conflict resolution" (ICR) Fisher means face-to-face, small group discussions between unofficial representatives of parties (from identity groups or states) that are engaged in destructive conflict; these discussions are aimed at conflict analysis and problem solving and are facilitated by an impartial third party of "scholar–practitioners." Fisher provides a precise date, locale, and founding ancestor for the birth of ICR: a "workshop" organized by John Burton and his colleagues in London, in December, 1965, to discuss a serious conflict involving Indonesia, Malaysia, and Singapore. The workshop, the first of several, lasted 5 days. When it was over, Fisher reports, "the delegates returned home and their respective governments reestablished diplomatic contact" (p. 23). This characterization, with its strongly implied but unstated causality, is telling. Supporters of ICR read it and can say, yes, of course, our primordial success. Skeptics (often political realists of the machtpolitik variety, with a strong commitment—if they be academics—to hypothesis testing) read it and seethe: How do we know the workshop had anything at all to do with reestablishing diplomatic contacts? Fisher is clearly among the supporters (indeed, among the formulators) of ICR; yet, one of the virtues of this important book is that he consistently tries to address the skeptics and "realists" on their own terms—through empirically-informed theory building, on the one hand, and process and outcome assessment and evaluation, on the other.

Thematically, the book is divided into three parts. (This parsing does not correspond to Fisher's own tripartite division, I should add.) The first part, mainly historical in organization, considers the development of ICR in terms of its key scholar–practitioners, among whom are the pioneering founders: John Burton,

Interactive Conflict Resolution, Ronald J. Fisher, 1997, Syracuse: Syracuse University Press, 1997.

Requests for reprints should be sent to Kevin Avruch, Department of Sociology and Anthropology (3G5), Fairfax, VA 2203. E-mail: kavruch@osf1.gmu.edu

Leonard Doob, and Herbert Kelman. Each person receives (and deserves) his own chapter, as does the late Edward Azar, who came from political science and international relations (rather than diplomacy or social psychology, as the first pioneers did), and offered, in his seminal notion of "protracted social conflicts," a critique of ICR's usual realist, power-based, and state-centered conflict theorizing, as well as a vocabulary for talking about the kinds of identity-based conflicts—ethnic, nationalist, religious—that state- and power-centered thinking is unable adequately to comprehend. Fisher does a masterful job of placing each in his own context—disciplinary, political, and personal—while tracing the incipient interconnections among them. Critical issues and reservations (focusing on theory or practice, or both) are introduced very early on and returned to throughout the book.

Moving out from the pioneers (but still very much part of the first theme of the work), Fisher then considers the work of other crucial figures, from the often underappreciated Bryant Wedge who, in addition to formulating a psychodynamic theory of ICR, was instrumental in founding the first postgraduate program in conflict resolution in the world in 1982, to Vamik Volkan and Joseph Montville, who joined a psychodynamic sensibility to concerns of firmly grounded practice, inventing (along with John McDonald and Louise Diamond) the notion of unofficial—second-track or multitrack—citizen diplomacy. Other figures contrast strikingly in their backgrounds and perspectives, from Quakers like Adam Curle and Mike Yarrow (who perforce stand outside "the system") to an ex-National Security Council and State Department senior official like Harold Saunders, who came to see the limitations that thinking solely within "the system" can impose. Along with a chapter on intercommunal "dialogue" groups (in the United States associated with Richard Schwartz and Louis Kriesberg, among others), Fisher succeeds in the book's first part in linking the growing variety of ICR theories and practices to a first-cut at the field's intellectual (and, to some extent, institutional) history.

In the book's second part, Fisher draws together in one conceptual package the varieties of conflict resolution theory and practice by developing, in two chapters, a model of third party consultation, of ICR "proper" (as defined in the beginning of this review), based upon the common characteristics and shared understandings of all the theory and practice discussed previously. Fisher's own contribution to the field—as a scholar–practitioner his published work dates back to 1972, placing him very close, in fact, to the founders' generation—lies primarily in his elucidation of the "contingency approach" to third party intervention, an approach that sensibly links the form of intervention (conciliation, consultation [ICR], arbitration, and peacekeeping) to the stage the parties to the conflict find themselves in (from discussion, polarization, and segregation, through to destruction). This allows Fisher to identify a particular stage in a conflict in which ICR has an especially important role to play: the prenegotiation stage, helping to facilitate what the late Jim Laue called "getting to the table."

The book's third part begins with the problem—alluded to earlier with reference to skeptical "hypothesis-testers"—of assessing or evaluating ICR practice. To date, most assessments have been based on case studies and are heavily anecdotal. Fisher recognizes that assessment and evaluation—process evaluation of course but equally so outcome evaluation—must proceed more rigorously in the future. This is so for two reasons: First, because ICR is part of a social science action research program and the canons of social scientific research demand it; secondly, because potential sponsors or patrons (foundations, universities, governments, or nongovernmental organizations [NGOs])—and "clients"—of ICR will reasonably demand it. The issue of sponsors and patrons leads Fisher finally to talk about the main problems facing ICR in the future: funding, training, institutionalization, and professionalization. In the ideal, universities will take the lead, among other reasons because, as Fisher writes, "it is essential that the research agenda not be allowed to wither away in the press for practice" (p. 256).

If we accept late 1965 as the birthdate of ICR, it is worth noting that it took more than 30 years for a book like Fisher's to appear. There have been a few very fine edited collections on ICR (as Fisher would define it), or conflict resolution in general, that bring together the views of different theorists, practitioners, or both under a more-or-less consistent editorial sensibility. The Sandole and van der Merwe (1993) volume or the various works of Bercovitch (e.g., 1996) on international mediation, come to mind. There have been also a number of book-length works by particular theorists and practitioners that prescriptively present their own views of how ICR should look—probably none more resolute than those of John Burton, already mentioned. What has been lacking, until now, is a comprehensive view of the field, one that combines a historical account of its development, a guide to its different practices, an analysis of the core features of third party consultation (the heart of ICR), and, not the least, a critical look at its limitations and the challenges it faces in the future. ICR provides all of this, making it a most significant—and, at 30-plus years, long overdue—book for both theorists and practitioners.

REFERENCES

Sandole, D. J. D., & Merwe, H. V. D. (Eds.). (1993). *Conflict resolution theory and practice: Integration and application.* Manchester, United Kingdom: Manchester University Press.

Bercovitch, J. (Ed.). (1996). *Resolving international conflicts: The theory and practice of mediation.* Boulder, CO: Rienner.

The grim fact is that we prepare for war like precocious giants and for peace like retarded pygmies.

Lester Pearson, 1955

PEACE AND CONFLICT: JOURNAL OF PEACE PSYCHOLOGY, 4(2), 191–192

Reducing Violence: A Mediator's View

Sheldon G. Levy

Psychology Department
Wayne State University

Adam Curle reflects on his past experience as a mediator to provide guidance for reducing violence. The work has three major sections: (a) a philosophical discussion of the psychological roots of violence and the impact of modern society, (b) direct mediation experiences of the author and principles of mediation, and (c) current peace-related activities with an emphasis on Osijek, Croatia.

Section 2 is the most valuable, notably, the chapters on soft and hard mediation. Here, the author develops, especially in the second of these, some important principles of mediation based on his personal experiences. Curle argues that modern economic–technological changes have resulted in a fundamental change in the psychological bases as well as the prevalence and intensity of violence. Quantitative studies of war, however, provide little evidence for an increase in modern times, particularly when overall population is considered (e.g, Richardson, 1960; Singer & Small, 1972). His points are worth consideration, but insufficient evidence is presented in support of the claims.

The philosophical underpinnings of the book tend to be only vaguely related to specific events and to individual actions that might further the goal of reducing violence. Nevertheless, the exploration of Tibetan–Buddhist principles has enlightening components, and the author makes a direct and cogent statement about economic injustice in the world and the policies of Western countries that are antithetical to human happiness. At times, this is accomplished in a stimulating literary style:

> The lunatic wars, the desperation, alienation, and despair are fed by the factories of
> the West, nourishing our over-fed society with the flesh and blood of the hungry. Our

---

Another Way: Positive response to contemporary violence, Adam Curle, 1995, Oxford, England: Jon Carpenter.

Requests for reprints should be sent to Sheldon Levy, 2951 Renfrew Street, Ann Arbor, Michigan 48105–1453. E-mail: shelly@umich.edu

predatory policies of profit at any price have richly manured the field in which the
seeds of future ethnic cleansing, cruelty, and conflict may grow. (p. 43)

Analytically, a number of questions may be raised. For example, the argument
against military intervention, as in Northern Ireland and Bosnia, fails to discuss the
potential outcome without intervention. The psychological roots of individual
violence are equated with those of intergroup violence, a debatable proposition; in
addition, the discussion of meaningless criminal violence in London and New York
might have been informed by some additional exploration of the reasons for the
differences in the magnitudes of homicide in the two cities.

Although well-written, the book has some other serious limitations. A major one
is the lack of theoretical integration. For example, the chapter on intervention and
interference is insufficiently related to the mediation principles, as are subsequent
descriptions of a number of current peace efforts among various centers. As a result,
the reader is unable to evaluate the particular programs, seminars, and workshops
that might be most valuable in developing peace–mediation efforts. It might be
hoped that Curle will pen a sequel, one that provides additional insights into the
mediation process and the psychology of mediation, an excellent core of which is
contained within the present work.

REFERENCES

Richardson, L. F. (1960). *Statistics of deadly quarrels*. Chicago: Quadrangle Books.
Singer, J. D., & Small, M. (1972). *The wages of war*. New York: Wiley.

PEACE AND CONFLICT: JOURNAL OF PEACE PSYCHOLOGY, 4(2), 193–195

New Thinking about War, Old Thinking about Peace

Gregory Hooks

Department of Sociology
Washington State University

It is doubtful that this book will have the impact of Alvin Toffler's earlier works. Nevertheless, the Tofflers's book on war is likely to be influential. The title is misleading because the book concentrates more on war than antiwar. Even when they do discuss peace making, the Tofflers endorse the United States as the leading military power and a "Reagan-esque" commitment to peace through strength. Whereas peace activists think peace requires disarmament and deemphasis of militarism, the Tofflers call on the United States to remain vigilant and to make the investments needed to remain the world's leading military power.

War and *Antiwar* builds on and extends the influential futurist perspective the Tofflers developed in previous books: *Future Shock, The Third Wave,* and *Powershift.* First Wave societies were founded on agriculture and brought about the transformation of human societies. Organized agriculture gave rise to the state and to the generation of a social surplus. Agricultural societies such as Ancient Egypt, China, Meso-America, and Mesopotamia are famous for cultural innovations such as writing, art, architecture, and codes of law. Although these civilizations were also innovative in warfare and conquest, military efforts "bore the unmistakable stamp of the First Wave agrarian economies that gave rise to them" (p. 40). "As was true in the economy, communications were primitive, and most orders were verbal, rather than written. The army, like the economy itself, lived off the land" (p. 39).

In the Tofflers's chronology, the Industrial Revolution set in motion a transition to Second Wave societies. Mass production became the foundation of production, whereas mass destruction was the hallmark of warfare. Whereas First Wave armies

---

War and Anti-War, Alvin Toffler & Heidi Toffler, 1993, Boston: Little, Brown.

Requests for reprints should be sent to Gregory Hooks, Department of Sociology, Washington State University, Pullman, WA 99164–4020.

were temporary organizations, Second Wave armies were large, specialized, permanent, and dramatically more lethal. World War I and World War II—the apex of Second Wave warfare—systematically mobilized the most productive societies to engage in prolonged and widespread destruction. Atomic weaponry enhanced the mass destruction of Second Wave warfare to the point that the central weapon could not be used without endangering the survival of the warring nations and all of humanity.

The current transition to Third Wave warfare is propelled by ongoing economic and social changes. Third Wave economies place greater stress on information and knowledge. By harnessing knowledge, corporations move from mass to flexible and rapidly changing production and marketing strategies. The emphasis on knowledge is reflected in the recruitment of staff, job expectations, work organization, the nature and terms of competition, and the societal infrastructure necessary to support economic activity. The changes in the economy are felt throughout society, including warfare. As knowledge becomes the cornerstone of military organization and effectiveness, the entire military organization is transformed. The absolute volume of goods needed in logistics support is reduced, but the materials provided must be of higher quality and appropriate for a given military operation. For instance, in place of tons of conventional bombs, a handful of smart bombs (i.e., bombs made more accurate by use of microelectronics) can destroy selected targets more accurately and efficiently. As the enhanced mobility and accuracy of weaponry makes possible deep strikes behind enemy lines, the frontline in a war becomes fuzzy and permeable. Whereas the ultimate Second Wave weapon—nuclear explosives—could not be used without endangering survival, the cutting edge Third Wave weapons are designed to be used because they provide the appropriate level and type of destructiveness. In an all-out war, the Third Wave battlefield is extended to include all areas of the belligerent nation, all parts of the globe, and quite possibly portions of outer space. The emphasis on knowledge over absolute size and volume is felt throughout the military organization. In a smaller military force, a larger number of military personnel are involved in maintaining weapons, whereas the total number of soldiers is much smaller.

The Tofflers provide an engaging and disturbing portrait of future warfare—made more interesting by glimpses of future technologies and interviews with military planners. They are critical of existing peace groups for opposing military spending, especially expenditures for military research and development (R & D). Despite the dangers posed by emerging technologies, the Tofflers are accepting of emerging military technologies, including the militarization of space. They advocate the development of new technologies and military organizations to sanitize and focus violence. Their futurist vision offers insights into emerging forms of warfare, terrorism, and antiterrorism and the role of the military in Third Wave societies.

Although the discussion of war is thorough, readers seeking insights and guidance toward the path of peace will be disappointed. The Tofflers devote their energies to exploring the changing technologies, planning, and organization for war. Moreover, despite repeated reference to its importance, they offer little new thinking into antiwar activity. They advocate "peace through strength" and urge the United States to maintain a lead in the development of military technology in order to ward off threats from terrorist organizations and irresponsible governments. The antiwar "activists" they highlight are military officers developing weapons to fight against terrorism or developing effective but relatively benign weapons to temporarily disable opponents. Thus, despite the emphasis on new thinking and new social arrangements, the Tofflers offer little hope that peace will be a part of our future and provide little guidance on the path to reach peace. The Tofflers fail to live up to the title's promise concerning antiwar thinking and strategies, but this readable and informative book makes a compelling case that war is being transformed. Although its answer is incomplete and unsatisfying, I recommend this book because it poses the challenge of developing new strategies for promoting peace as war is transformed.

REFERENCES

Toffler, A. (1970). *Future shock.* New York: Bantam.

Toffler, A. (1980). *The third wave.* New York: Morrow.

Toffler, A. (1990). *Powershift: Knowledge, wealth, and violence at the edge of the 21st century.* New York: Bantam.

Peace Education
in a Postmodern World

Issue Editor:
Ian M. Harris

Peabody Journal of Education
Volume 71, Number 3, 1996

LEA LAWRENCE ERLBAUM ASSOCIATES, PUBLISHERS
Mahwah, New Jersey

PEACE EDUCATION IN A POSTMODERN WORLD
A Special Issue of the Peabody Journal of Education

guest editor:
Ian M. Harris
University of Wisconsin, Milwaukee

This special issue of the *Peabody Journal of Education* provides a comprehensive overview of the latest developments in peace education reform. School reforms based upon principles of peace education have in common a belief in the power of peace to create a positive learning climate in schools and to address the problems of violence in the broader culture. A peace education strategy for improving school productivity rests upon three main assumptions:

1. Violence contributes to the poor performance of many students.
2. Adults in school settings need to address problems created by violence in order for schools to improve.
3. Anxieties that make it hard for students to master traditional subject matter can best be addressed by a comprehensive peace education strategy that makes school a safe place to learn and provides students with knowledge about alternative nonviolent ways to resolve conflicts.

Peace building reforms go beyond responding to immediate forms of violence that may be overwhelming students and teachers to promoting positive images of peace through the study of nonviolence. Written by established experts in the field of peace education from six different countries, this collection of articles not only represents a wide variety of peace education practices from different corners of the globe, but it also represents varying academic perspectives. The articles in this issue were collected at the Peace Education Commission sessions during the International Peace Research Association conference held in Malta in 1994. Educators can play a key role in helping human societies progress toward more sustainable ways of living by implementing peacemaking, peacekeeping, and peace building strategies in school programs. Peace education reforms point to a new way of thinking about schools as vehicles for promoting a peace culture through insights offered by nonviolent theory.

0-8058-9912-X [paper] / 1996 / 192pp. / $20.00
No further discounts apply.

Prices subject to
change without notice.

Lawrence Erlbaum Associates, Inc.
10 Industrial Avenue, Mahwah, NJ 07430
201/236-9500   FAX 201/236-0072

Call toll-free to order: 1-800-9-BOOKS-9...9am to 5pm EST only.
e-mail to: orders@erlbaum.com
visit LEA's web site at http://www.erlbaum.com